When they had heard the king, they departed; and, lo, the star, which they saw in the east, went before them, till it came and stood over where the young child was.

When they saw the star, they rejoiced with exceeding great joy.

And when they were come into the house, they saw the young child with Mary, his mother, and fell down, and worshipped him; and when they had opened their treasures, they presented unto him gifts: gold, and frankincense, and myrrh.

And being warned of God in a dream that they should not return to Herod, they departed into their own country another way.

And when they were departed, behold, the angel of the Lord appeareth to Joseph in a dream, saying, Arise, and take the young child and his mother, and flee into Egypt, and be thou there until I bring thee word; for Herod will seek the young child to destroy him.

When he arose, he took the young child and his mother by night, and departed into Egypt:

And was there until the death of Herod, that it might be fulfilled which was spoken by the Lord through the prophet, saying, Out of Egypt have I called my son.

An Oxford Book of
Christmas Stories

*This collection is for
my mother and father*

An Oxford Book of
CHRISTMAS STORIES

Dennis Pepper

Oxford University Press
Oxford Toronto Melbourne

Oxford University Press, Walton Street, Oxford OX2 6DP

Oxford New York Toronto
Delhi Bombay Calcutta Madras Karachi
Petaling Jaya Singapore Hong Kong Tokyo
Nairobi Dar es Salaam Cape Town
Melbourne Auckland

and associated companies in
Beirut Berlin Ibadan Nicosia

Oxford is a trade mark of Oxford University Press

ISBN 0 19 2781197

British Library Cataloguing in Publication Data

An Oxford book of Christmas stories.
1. Children's stories, English
2. Christmas stories
I. Pepper, Dennis
823'.01'0833 PZ5

ISBN 0-19-278119-7

The illustrations are by:
Judy Brown, Graham Clapham, Helen Clipson, Penny Dann,
Simon Dorrell, Terry Gabbey, Fred Gambino, Gerard Gibson,
Robert Goldsmith, Jonathan Heap, Chris Hill, Tudor Humphries,
Robin Jacques, Kevin Lyles, Ian Miller, David Parkins, Susan Scott,
and Martin White.

Set by Oxford Publishing Services, Oxford
Printed in Hong Kong

Contents

Grandfather Frost

James Riordan

There once lived an old man with his second wife, and they each had a daughter. The wife pampered her own daughter, who was lazy and bad-tempered. But she was unkind to her stepdaughter.

The old man's daughter had to rise before daybreak to tend the cattle, fetch the firewood, light the stove and sweep the floor. Yet her stepmother found fault with all she did and grumbled at her the whole day through.

Even the wildest wind grows calm with time, but there was no quieting the old woman once she was roused. She would not be content until she had driven the poor girl from the house.

'Get rid of her, old man,' she said one day to her husband. 'I cannot bear the sight of her any longer. Drive her into the forest and leave her in the snow.'

The old man pleaded but the wife always had her way. So, one bitterly cold morning, he harnessed his horses to the sledge and called his daughter:

'Come, my child, we are going for a ride, climb into the sledge.'

The sledge raced over the crisp snow into the forest until it came to a lofty fir-tree. There the old man stopped and left the luckless girl trembling by a deep snowdrift. He drove home with heavy heart, certain he would never see his daughter again.

It was very cold, and the girl sat beneath the hoary fir-tree shivering. All of a sudden, she caught her breath, for she could hear a cracking and snapping of twigs, and she knew Grandfather Frost was leaping through the trees. In a twinkling he was in the topmost branches of the very tree by which she sat.

'Are you warm, my pretty one?' he called.

'Yes, quite warm, thank you, Grandfather Frost,' she answered.

He came down lower and the cracking and snapping grew louder than ever.

'Are you warm?' he called again. 'Are you snug, my pretty one?'

The girl was scarcely able to catch her breath, but she said:

'Yes, I'm quite warm, thank you, Grandfather Frost.'

He then climbed lower still, cracking and snapping the frosty boughs very loudly indeed.

'Are you warm?' he asked. 'Are you snug, my pretty one? Are you cosy, my sweet snow child?'

The girl was growing numb and could hardly move her tongue, but still she managed to whisper:

'I'm quite warm, thank you, Grandfather Frost.'

Then Grandfather Frost took pity on the girl and wrapped her in his fluffy furs and fleecy eiderdowns.

Meanwhile the wicked stepmother was frying pancakes and preparing for the funeral repast. She said to her husband:

'Go to the forest, old fool, and bring your daughter back to be buried!'

The old man harnessed the horses and obediently went into the forest and there found his daughter on the very spot where he had left her. She was alive and well, wrapped in a warm sable coat over a glittering velvet gown. Beside her stood a large chest stuffed with furs and rare gems.

The old man was overjoyed. He seated his daughter in the sledge, put the chest in beside her and drove home.

Back in the house the old woman was still frying pancakes when, suddenly, her little dog began to bark:

'Ruff-ruff! The old man's daughter comes rich and fair,
A wondrous fortune found she there!'

The old woman threw the dog a pancake and said:
'You are wrong, dog! You should say:

"The old man's daughter is cold and dead,
The forest snow lies on her head!"'

The dog munched the pancake, but still barked:

'Ruff-ruff! The old man's daughter comes rich and fair,
A wondrous fortune found she there!'

The old woman hurled more pancakes at the dog and, when this did not stop it, she beat it until it ran howling into the snow.

Suddenly there came the sound of the sledge racing into the yard; the door burst open and in walked the old man's daughter, dazzling in her white furs and precious stones. Behind her walked her happy father bearing the heavy chest of furs and jewels. The old woman was astonished to see her alive and dressed in such finery.

'Harness the horses, old man!' she said to her husband. 'Take my own daughter to the forest and leave her at the same spot.'

The old man put the woman's daughter into the sledge, drove her into the forest and left her by the deep snowdrift under the lofty fir-tree. She was soon so cold her teeth chattered and her feet grew numb.

Presently Grandfather Frost came leaping through the treetops, cracking and snapping the twigs, and stopped to ask the old woman's daughter:

'Are you warm, my pretty one?'

'Oh no, I'm terribly cold!' she snapped. 'Don't pinch and pierce me so!'

Grandfather Frost came lower, making the branches snap and crackle more loudly.

'Are you warm?' he called. 'Are you snug, my pretty one?'

'Oh no, I'm freezing!' she snapped back. 'Go away, you stupid old man!'

But Grandfather Frost came down still lower and the branches cracked and snapped louder than ever and his breath grew colder and colder.

'Are you warm?' he called again. 'Are you snug, my pretty one? Are you cosy, my sweet one?'

'Oh no!' she cried. 'I'm frozen stiff! Go away, you stupid grey-beard!'

Grandfather Frost was so cross that he sent a piercing cold blast through her and turned the old woman's daughter into a block of ice.

Day had barely dawned when the old woman said to her husband:

'Make haste and harness the horses, old man. Go and fetch my daughter and bring her back clad in furs and jewels.'

When the old man had gone, the little dog began to bark:

> *'Ruff-ruff! The old man's daughter will soon be wed,*
> *But the old woman's daughter is cold and dead!'*

The old woman threw the dog a pie and said:
'You are wrong, dog! You should say:

> *"The old woman's daughter comes rich and fair,*
> *A wondrous fortune found she there."'*

The dog continued its barking:

> *'Ruff-ruff! The old woman's daughter is cold and dead!'*

Before long she heard the sound of horses' hoofs and rushed out to greet her daughter. But, when the old woman turned back the cover on the sledge, she found her daughter frozen stiff. So overcome with grief was she that she died.

The old man and his daughter lived on together happily for many years, well rid of the cruel old woman and her lazy daughter.

The Snow-man

Mabel Marlowe

A snow-man once stood upon a hill, with his face towards the sunset. A very fine snow-man he was, as tall as a soldier, and much fatter. He had two pieces of glass for eyes, and a stone for a nose, and a piece of black wood for a mouth, and in his hand he held a stout, knobbly club.

But he had no clothes at all, not even a hat, and the wind on the top of that hill was as bitter as wind could be.

'How cold I am! I am as cold as ice,' said the snow-man. 'But that red sky looks warm.' So he lifted his feet from the ground, and went tramp, tramp, tramping down the slope towards the setting sun.

Very soon he overtook a gipsy woman, who was wearing a bright red shawl. 'Ha, that looks warm! I must have it,' thought the snow-man. So he went up to the gipsy woman and he said, 'Give me that red shawl.'

'No, indeed! I cannot spare it on this wintry day,' answered the gipsy. 'I am cold enough as it is.'

'Cold!' shouted the snow-man in a very growlish voice. 'Are you as cold as I am, I wonder! Are you cold inside as well as outside? Are you made of ice, through and through and through?'

'No, I suppose not,' mumbled the gipsy, who was getting hot with fright.

'Then give me your red shawl this moment, or I shall strike you with my stout, knobbly club.'

Then the gipsy took off her red shawl, grumbling all the time, and gave it to the snow-man. He put it round his shoulders, without a word of thanks, and went tramp, tramp, tramping down the hill. And the shivering gipsy followed behind him.

Presently the snow-man overtook a ploughboy who was wearing his grandmother's long, red woollen mittens.

'Ha, they look warm! I must have them,' thought the snow-

11

man. So he went up to the ploughboy and he said, 'Give me those red woollen mittens.'

'No, indeed!' said the ploughboy. 'They belong to my grandmother. She lent them to me because my fingers were so cold.'

'Cold!' shouted the snow-man, in a very roarish voice. 'Are your fingers as cold as mine, I wonder! Are your hands and arms frozen into ice, through and through and through?'

'No, I suppose not,' mumbled the ploughboy.

'Then give me those red mittens, this moment, or I shall strike you with my stout, knobbly club.'

So the ploughboy drew off the warm mittens, grumbling all the time, and the snow-man put them on, without a word of thanks. Then he went tramp, tramp, tramping down the hill. And the gipsy and the ploughboy followed him.

After a while he overtook a tame pirate, wearing a pirate's thick red cap, with a tassel dangling down his back.

'Ha! That looks warm! I must have it,' said the snow-man. So he went up to the tame pirate and he said, 'Give me that red tassel cap.'

'No, indeed!' said the pirate. 'A nice cold in the head I should get if I did.'

'Cold in the head!' shouted the snow-man, in a very thunderish voice. 'Is your head as cold as mine, I wonder! Are your brains made of snow, and your bones solid ice, through and through and through?'

'No, I suppose not,' muttered the tame pirate.

'Then give me that red tassel cap, this moment, or I shall set upon you with my stout, knobbly club.'

Now the pirate felt very sorry that he had turned tame, but he did not like the look of that knobbly stick, so he gave up his red tassel cap. The snow-man put it on without a word of thanks. Then he went tramp, tramp, tramping down the hill, with the tassel bumping up and down. And the gipsy woman, and the ploughboy, and the tame pirate followed him.

At last he reached the bottom of the hill, where the village school house stood, and there was the village schoolmaster on the doorstep, looking at the sunset. He was smoking a glowing briar pipe, and on his feet were two red velvet slippers.

'Ha, those look warm! I must have them,' said the snow-man.

So he went up to the schoolmaster and said, 'Give me those red slippers.'

'Certainly, if you want them,' said the schoolmaster. 'Take them by all means. It is far too cold today to be tramping about with bare toes,' and he stooped and drew off his slippers, and there he stood in some bright red socks, thick and woolly and knitted by hand.

'Ha! Those look warm! Give them to me!' said the snow-man.

'Certainly, if you want them,' said the schoolmaster. 'But you must come inside. I cannot take my socks off here, in the doorway. Come on to the mat.'

So the snow-man stepped inside the doorway, and stood upon the mat.

'Be sharp with those socks. My feet are as cold as solid ice,' he grumbled.

'I am sorry to hear that,' said the schoolmaster. 'But I have a warm red blanket airing over the stove. Come in, sir. Sit on that chair by the fire, sir. Put your cold feet upon this snug red footstool, and let me wrap this red blanket around your legs.'

So the snow-man came into the schoolhouse, and sat upon a chair by the glowing fire, and put his feet upon the red footstool, and the schoolmaster wrapped the red blanket round and round and round his legs. (And all this while the gipsy woman, and the ploughboy, and the tame pirate were peering in at the window.)

'Are you feeling warmer?' asked the schoolmaster.

'No. I am as cold as an iceberg.'

'Come closer to the fire.'

So the schoolmaster pushed the chair closer to the fire, but the snow-man gave him not one word of thanks.

'Are you feeling warmer now?'

'No. I am as cold as a stone. My feet feel like icy water.'

'Move closer to the fire,' said the schoolmaster, and he pushed the chair right against the kerb. 'There! Are you warmer now?'

'No, no, no! I am colder than ever. I cannot feel my feet at all. I cannot feel my legs at all. I cannot feel my back at all.'

Then the schoolmaster pushed the chair quite close up against the stove. 'Are you warmer now?' he said.

But there was no answer, except a slithery sliding sound, and the drip, drip, drip of black snow-water.

'Dear me!' whispered the snow-man, in a gurgling kind of

voice. 'I have dropped my stout, knobbly club. My red slippers are floating into the ashpan. My mittens are swimming in a little river on the floor. My shawl is gone. My red tassel cap is slipping— slipping away. My head is going . . . going . . .'

Splosh! Splash! Gurgle!

'That's the end of him,' said the schoolmaster, and he went to fetch the mop.

Then the gipsy woman, and the ploughboy and the tame pirate came in and picked up their things, and wrung them out, and dried them at the stove, and the schoolmaster put his red slippers on the hearth, and hung the red blanket over the back of the chair.

Then he picked up the stout, knobbly club and gave the fire a poke.

Mr Pickwick on the Ice

Charles Dickens

Mr Weller and the fat boy, having by their joint endeavours cut out a slide, were exercising themselves thereupon in a very masterly and brilliant manner. Sam Weller, in particular, was displaying that beautiful feat of fancy sliding which is currently denominated 'knocking at the cobbler's door', and which is achieved by skimming over the ice on one foot, and occasionally giving a twopenny postman's knock upon it with the other. It was a good long slide, and there was something in the motion which Mr Pickwick, who was very cold with standing still, could not help envying.

'It looks nice, warm exercise that, doesn't it?' he inquired of Wardle.

'Ah, it does indeed,' replied Wardle. 'Do you slide?'

'I used to do so, on the gutters, when I was a boy,' replied Mr Pickwick.

'Try it now,' said Wardle.

'Oh, do, please, Mr Pickwick!' cried all the ladies.

'I should be very happy to afford you any amusement,' replied Mr Pickwick, 'but I haven't done such a thing these thirty years.'

'Pooh! pooh! Nonsense!' said Wardle. 'Here; I'll keep you company. Come along!' And away went the good-tempered old fellow down the slide, with a rapidity which came very close upon Mr Weller, and beat the fat boy all to nothing.

Mr Pickwick paused, considered, pulled off his gloves and put them in his hat; took two or three short runs, balked himself as often, and at last took another run, and went slowly and gravely down the slide, with his feet about a yard and a quarter apart, amidst the gratified shouts of all the spectators.

'Keep the pot a-bilin', sir!' said Sam; and down went Wardle again, and then Mr Pickwick, and then Sam, and then Mr Winkle, and then Mr Bob Sawyer, and then the fat boy, and then Mr

Snodgrass, following closely upon each other's heels, and running after each other with as much eagerness as if all their future prospects in life depended on their expedition.

It was the most intensely interesting thing to observe the manner in which Mr Pickwick performed his share in the ceremony; to watch the torture of anxiety with which he viewed the person behind, gaining upon him at the imminent hazard of tripping him up; to see him gradually expend the painful force which he had put on at first, and turn slowly round on the slide, with his face towards the point from which he had started; to contemplate the playful smile which mantled on his face when he had accomplished the distance, and the eagerness with which he turned round when he had done so and ran after his predecessor—his black gaiters tripping pleasantly through the snow, and his eyes beaming cheerfulness and gladness through his spectacles. And when he was knocked down (which happened upon the average every third round), it was the most invigorating sight that can possibly be imagined to behold him gather up his hat, gloves, and handkerchief, with a glowing countenance, and resume his station in the rank with an ardour and enthusiasm that nothing could abate.

The sport was at its height, the sliding was at the quickest, the laughter was at the loudest, when a sharp, smart crack was heard. There was a quick rush towards the bank, a wild scream from the ladies, and a shout from Mr Tupman. A large mass of ice disappeared; the water bubbled up over it; Mr Pickwick's hat, gloves, and handkerchief were floating on the surface; and this was all of Mr Pickwick that anybody could see.

Dismay and anguish were depicted on every countenance; the males turned pale, and the females fainted; Mr Snodgrass and Mr Winkle grasped each other by the hand, and gazed at the spot where their leader had gone down, with frenzied eagerness; while Mr Tupman, by way of rendering the promptest assistance, and at the same time conveying to any persons who might be within hearing the clearest possible notion of the catastrophe, ran off across the country at his utmost speed, screaming 'Fire!' with all his might.

It was at this very moment, when old Wardle and Sam Weller were approaching the hole with cautious steps, and Mr Benjamin Allen was holding a hurried consultation with Mr Bob Sawyer on

17

the advisability of bleeding the company generally, as an improving little bit of professional practice—it was at this very moment that a face, head, and shoulders emerged from beneath the water, and disclosed the features and spectacles of Mr Pickwick.

'Keep yourself up for an instant—for only one instant!' bawled Mr Snodgrass.

'Yes, do; let me implore you—for my sake!' roared Mr Winkle, deeply affected. The adjuration was rather unnecessary—the probability being that if Mr Pickwick had declined to keep himself up for anybody else's sake, it would have occurred to him that he might as well do so for his own.

'Do you feel the bottom there, old fellow?' said Wardle.

'Yes, certainly,' replied Mr Pickwick, wringing the water from his head and face, and gasping for breath. 'I fell upon my back. I couldn't get on my feet at first.'

The clay upon so much of Mr Pickwick's coat as was yet visible bore testimony to the accuracy of this statement; and as the fears of the spectators were still further relieved by the fat boy's suddenly recollecting that the water was nowhere more than five feet deep, prodigies of valour were performed to get him out. After a vast quantity of splashing, and cracking, and struggling, Mr Pickwick was at length fairly extricated from his unpleasant position, and once more stood on dry land.

'Oh, he'll catch his death of cold,' said Emily.

'Dear old thing!' said Arabella. 'Let me wrap this shawl round you, Mr Pickwick.'

'Ah, that's the best thing you can do,' said Wardle; 'and when you've got it on, run home as fast as your legs can carry you, and jump into bed directly.'

A dozen shawls were offered on the instant. Three or four of the thickest having been selected, Mr Pickwick was wrapped up, and started off, under the guidance of Mr Weller—presenting the singular phenomenon of an elderly gentleman, dripping wet, and without a hat, with his arms bound down to his sides, skimming over the ground, without any clearly-defined purpose, at the rate of six good English miles an hour.

But Mr Pickwick cared not for appearances in such an extreme case, and urged on by Sam Weller, he kept at the very top of his speed until he reached the door of Manor Farm, where Mr Tupman had arrived some five minutes before, and had frightened the old lady into palpitations of the heart by impressing her with the unalterable conviction that the kitchen chimney was on fire—a calamity which always presented itself in glowing colours to the old lady's mind when anybody about her evinced the smallest agitation.

Mr Pickwick paused not an instant until he was snug in bed.

Sliding

Leslie Norris

The cold had begun very suddenly on Tuesday night, when Bernard had gone out to play. The boys were playing kick-the-tin in the lamplight at the top of the street, and nobody realized how cold it was until Randall Jenkins went home for his cap and scarf. Then they all felt the bitter weather—at their knees, their wrists, the tips of their ears. Bernard went indoors and borrowed his father's knitted scarf and found his own old gloves from last winter. Pretty soon, the game was on again and they forgot about the weather.

That night in bed, the sheets were hard and slippery, unfriendly as ice. Carefully, by an act of will, Bernard made warm a place in bed exactly the same shape as his body, thin and hunched under the covers. He extended it gradually, inch by inch, sending his toes gently into the cold until at last he was straight and comfortable. Everything was fine then, except that he had to pull the blankets firmly about his ears and shoulders. In the morning, the window was covered with frost flowers, and the kitchen fire blazed ferociously against the Welsh winter. He called for Danny Kenyon, as usual, on the way to school. Danny was his best friend, and they ran all the way, although Danny was short and plump.

Bernard was used now to the ice. Out in the yard, the tap had been frozen for days and a tongue of glass poked out of its mouth. Every morning was grey and spiteful, churlish light making the whole world dingy. Patches of hard grit gathered in the gutters and at the corners of streets, whipping against the boy's face and into his eyes. All day long, the shops kept their lights on, but there was nothing cheerful about them; only Mr Toomey's shop was strong with colour, because of the brilliant globes of his pyramids of oranges.

In school on Friday morning, Albert Evans began to cry. The

teacher asked him why, but Albert wouldn't answer. It was Randall Jenkins who told about Albert's legs. The inside of his thighs was chafed raw—red all the way from his groin to his knees. The skin was hard and angry, and there were weeping cracks in it. The teacher let Albert sit in front, near the stove, and he didn't have to do any arithmetic. When Bernard told his mother about Albert's legs, she narrowed her mouth and said that Annie Evans had no more sense than the day she was born, and then she took a pot of ointment over to Albert's house.

While she was out, Bernard's father told him it had been the coldest day in more than twenty years. It was funny about skin and cold weather. Some boys turned red because of the cold, and some rather blue, and Danny Kenyon's knees went a kind of mottled colour—but he only laughed. When Bernard's mother came back, she was vexed. 'Poor little scamp,' she said. 'It's agony for him to walk at all.'

After breakfast on Saturday morning, Bernard climbed into his den, which was the room above the stable in the yard. His father had whitewashed the walls for him, and together they'd carried up some old chairs from the house. Two large kitchen tables, covered with paints and bits of models and old newspapers, stood side by side under the windows. His record-player was there, too, and it was warm because of the oilstove. It was a fine room, with an enormous spider in the corner of the roof and a web thick and black against the white wall.

Bernard sat in a chair near the stove and began to think of the things he would do when the summer came and he would be nine, going on ten. He and Danny Kenyon would go camping, they would find a field that nobody else knew about, and every day would be cloudless. He made the field in his head—the perfect green of its grass, its great protective tree in one corner, and its stream so pure that you could see every fragmentary pebble, every waving strand of weed in its bed. They were too young to go camping. He knew that.

And then Randall Jenkins climbed the stairs. He was grinning. He carried about his neck a pair of heavy boots, tied by their laces. He took them off and dropped them proudly on the floor, where they stood bluntly on their uncouth soles, exactly as if they still had someone's feet in them and invisible legs climbing up from them. Randall held out his hands to the stove and danced slowly around it, revolving so that he warmed himself all over.

'Coming sliding?' he said. 'This afternoon? We're all going–on the big pond; it's holding.'

'I'll ask,' said Bernard. 'I expect it will be all right.'

He thought of the big pond under the hills, its heavy acres hundreds of yards wide, the water cold and thick. It held in its silence fabulous pike, more than a yard long and twenty pounds in weight, although Bernard had never seen one. He didn't like the big pond.

'You'll need special boots,' said Randall. 'I've borrowed my brother's–take a look at them.'

He lifted the great boots and held them for Bernard's inspection. The soles were an inch thick and covered with a symmetrical pattern of bold nails–flat squares shining like silver. Crescents of smooth metal were screwed at heel and toe into the leather, the edges worn thin as a razor.

Randall rubbed his sleeve over the scarred toe caps, breathing on them as he burnished.

'These are the ones,' he said. 'My brother's old working boots. They might have been made for sliding.'

'They're too big for you,' said Bernard.

'Size 7,' said Randall with satisfaction. 'My brother's grown out of them. Three or four pairs of socks and they'll fit me–you watch. I'll scream right across the pond.'

He moved the boots through the air as if they were fighter planes.

'You'll need a pair like this,' he said. 'Otherwise you'll never go any distance.'

Randall was lucky to have big brothers. Bernard thought dismally of his own boots–light, gentlemanly, with rubber soles and heels. His grandfather didn't like rubber soles and heels, either. Only thieves and policemen, he had said, two classes of society with much in common, wear rubber on their feet. Bernard didn't understand that.

'Is Danny Kenyon coming?' Bernard asked.

'Sure,' Randall said. 'We're all going. I told you.'

After lunch, they all went to the pond, protected by layers of clothing against the wind's knives, their woollen hats pulled over their ears. Some of the boys had managed to borrow heavy boots,

just to be like Randall Jenkins, and they clumped awkwardly up the hill as they learned to manage their erratic feet. Randall Jenkins turned out his toes, shuffling around corners like Charlie Chaplin, and they all laughed.

Bernard began to feel very happy. He began to imagine the long quietness of his gliding over the ice. He thought of thick ice, clear as glass, beneath which the cold fish swam, staring up with their goggle eyes at the sliding boys. He thought of ice like a dazzling mirror set in the hills, on which they could skim above their own images, each brilliant slider like two perfect boys–one upside down–joined at the feet. In his happiness he jostled and bumped against Danny Kenyon, and Danny charged right back at him, until they were both laughing and the wind blew away their white breath in clouds from their mouths.

But the pond was disappointment. Winter had taken all the life from the hills, and the face of the ice was grey and blind–the colour of the flat sky above it. There were no reeds at the lake's edge. Featureless, the ice stretched on, swept by an unhindered

24

wind. The boys bent their heads down against the brutal cold. Their voices were feeble; they felt small and helpless. Only Randall Jenkins was unaffected. Whooping and waving at the ice, he began to run, lifting his enormous boots in slow, high-stepping strides. He ran on, planting his laughable feet one after the other so heavily that Bernard imagined he could hear the whole bowl ringing; and then, his legs rigid, both arms raised for balance, he slid with comic dignity. They all rushed after him, sliding and calling. The afternoon was suddenly warm and vigorous.

Bernard was a good runner, and he hurled himself along so that the momentum of his first slide would be memorable. He raced past two or three of the boys and then stopped, his legs braced wide, head up, arms raised. He was expecting something birdlike, something approaching flight, but nothing happened. His rubber soles clung wickedly to the surface of the ice and he slid no more than a few yards. He was inconsolable.

He shuffled cautiously along the margins of the ice, tentative and humble. Far out, in the wide middle of the pond, he could see the dark figures of his friends, freely sliding, gyrating, crouching, skating on one leg. Their voices came bouncing to him high and clear like the calling of seagulls. But he ran alone at the edge of the lake, unable to slide. Then, unexpectedly, without warning, he found himself free of the binding friction that had held him. He had begun to glide. He sat on the bank, lifted one foot, and inspected the sole of his boot. A thin layer of polished ice, thinner than a postage stamp, had built itself onto the black rubber. He saw that the other boot was also transformed, and he ran jubilantly into the heart of the pond, far outstripping the loud boys, sliding far and fast, hearing their admiration and surprise. The pond was his.

Late in the afternoon came two young men, tall, with deep voices, all of seventeen years old. They strapped on their sharp and proper skates, and skated expertly. Briefly, the boys watched them, but soon Randall Jenkins had organized a game of follow-my-leader. Randall was a superb leader, his invention and audacity encouraging them to a skill and daring they had not known they possessed. The last dare was to run as fast as they could toward the ice from the shore itself, leaping from the bank at full speed. Randall raced forward, his long slow legs gathering pace as he ran, and then he leaped high outward from the bank, landing yards out. Rigid as a scarecrow, he sped on, stopping at last a prodigious way out, and standing absolutely still in the attitude of his sliding. One by one they followed him, although nobody was as brave as Randall, nobody would hurl himself as uninhibitedly from the steep bank. At last, only three boys were left.

Bernard thought he had never seen anything as lovely as the dark ice, hardly lit at all as the light faded, and the still figures of his friends dotted about on it, not moving, their arms in a variety of postures, their bodies bent or upright. He took a great breath, and ran. He had never felt so light, he was full of fiery energy. He reached the bank and thrust himself so urgently, so powerfully, that the exhilaration of his leap made him gasp. He hit the ice beautifully, and felt at once the speed of his sliding, and he knew that nobody had ever slid so far. Stopping at last, he looked around. He was yards farther than Randall Jenkins, miles farther than the other boys. Jackie Phelps was slowing miserably a long way off, and only Danny was left to jump.

He could see Danny up on the bank, preparing to run, swaying from one foot to the other, bent forward at the waist. Cupping his hands, Bernard shouted, 'You'll never reach me!'

Danny waved furiously. You could see that he was going to give it all he had by the way he set his shoulders. He ran forward and leaped wildly from the bank. Bernard could see him so clearly that everything seemed to happen in slow motion. He saw Danny hit the ice and knew that it was wrong. Danny landed on his heels, not on the flat of his feet, and his body was already tilting gently backward. He sped along, the slope of his body already irrevocably past the point of recovery. They saw his heels leave the ice, and for a perceptible moment he sailed through the unsupporting air before the back of his head cracked frighteningly against the surface. He lay broken and huddled. Bernard could not move. He could see Danny in a black heap, but he couldn't move toward him. It was Randall Jenkins who reached him first, and they all ran in behind him.

They crowded around Danny, looking down at him. His face was still and white, his eyes closed. As they looked, a little worm of blood appeared at one nostril and curled onto Danny's lip. What if he should die? Bernard bent, and in an urgency of terror lifted his friend. Randall helped him, and together they hauled Danny to the bank. Some of the boys were crying, and Randall set them to collect twigs, pieces of paper—anything that would burn. Bernard took off Danny's gloves and rubbed his hands in his own. Danny's fingers were very cold, but in a while he began to move and groan. Twice he opened his eyes, without recognizing them and without saying anything.

Randall lit a fire, and it burned with a dull light, sullenly. He sent all the boys except Bernard to find more fuel, told them to rip branches from small trees. Bernard wiped the blood from Danny's nose, and after a while the bleeding stopped. It hadn't been very much, he comforted himself. His knees hurt from bending down so long. Behind him, Randall had whipped the fire into a huge blaze that pushed away the darkness, and the boys sat near it, not speaking. Danny moved heavily, sat up, and looked at Bernard.

'Oh, my God,' said Danny Kenyon. 'What happened?'

He was all right; everything was all right. The boys cheered, slapped each other on the back, put Danny to sit even nearer the fire. They danced and sang, released from fright, and they were

27

pert and arrogant when one of the young men suddenly appeared.

'What's the matter with him?' he asked, bending over Danny.

'Nothing,' said Randall airily. 'Nothing at all.'

'None of your business,' said Jackie Phelps, out of the darkness.

'How old are you?' said the young man to Bernard.

'Ten,' lied Bernard. He pointed to Randall. 'And he's eleven,' he said.

'Get that boy home,' said the young man. 'How do you feel, son?'

'Great,' said Danny. 'I feel great.'

'Get home,' said the young man. 'And the rest of you see that this fire is out.'

He skated into the darkness. Bernard could feel the iron shearing of his blades.

The fire was very hot. Bernard could imagine it warming a thin crust of frozen soil, then maybe deeper, a half inch deep. Already he could hear the ice hiss in the released ground. He sat with his

back up against Danny's back, so they were both comfortable. All the boys sat around. They were very quiet.

Bit by bit, the dark and the cold crept into the interstices of the flames, winning the night back for winter. Randall got up and stamped about. His feet had gone to sleep.

'Time to go, lads,' he said. 'Time to go.'

They stood up and followed obediently behind Randall. Bernard was so tired that his legs were slow and stiff, and his mind was always about two steps in front of them, but in a little while they got better. The boys went down the lane past the old rectory and started down the hill towards the town. A night wind flew at them as if it cared nothing for people and meant to blow straight through them. Bernard began to shiver. What if Danny had died? He saw again Danny's face as he lay on the ice, as white and stiff as a candle. As he looked, an imaginary worm of blood crawled from Danny's nose and covered the side of his cheek. He closed his mind from the terror of it and put his arm over Danny's shoulder.

'How do you feel?' he whispered, but Randall heard him.

'He feels great,' Randall Jenkins roared, his voice red as fire. 'What's the matter with you? He feels fine!'

'I'm OK,' said Danny. 'Honest, I'm OK.'

A few small flakes of snow fell out of the sky. The boys felt them hit their faces, light as cobwebs, and then vanish. It was intolerably dark and cold. As they entered the first streets of the town, the boys moved together for solace and started to run. They trotted close together, moving home as one boy through the darkness, united against whatever terror might threaten them.

Father Christmas and Father Christmas

David Henry Wilson

Jeremy James first met Father Christmas one Saturday morning in a big shop. He was a little surprised to see him there, because it was soon going to be Christmas, and Jeremy James thought Santa Claus really ought to be somewhere in the North Pole filling sacks with presents and feeding his reindeer. However, there he was, on a platform in the toy department, handing out little parcels to the boys and girls who came to see him.

'Here you are, Jeremy James,' said Daddy, and handed him a 50p piece.

'What's that for?' asked Jeremy James.

'To give to Santa Claus,' said Daddy. 'You have to pay to go and see him. I'll wait for you here.'

Daddy stood rocking the twins in the pram, while Jeremy James joined the end of a long queue of children (Mummy was busy wasting time in the food department). Jeremy James thought it rather odd that you had to pay for Santa Claus. It was as if Santa Claus was a bar of chocolate or a packet of liquorice all-sorts.

'Do we really have to pay 50p to see him?' he asked a tall boy in front of him.

'Yeah,' said the tall boy. 'An' he'll prob'ly give you a plastic car worth 5p.'

Jeremy James stood on tiptoe to try and catch a glimpse of Father Christmas. He could just see him, all wrapped up in his red cloak and hood, talking to a little girl with pigtails. It certainly was him—there was no mistaking the long white beard and the rosy cheeks. It was really quite an honour that Santa Claus should have come to this particular shop out of all the shops in the world, and perhaps he needed the 50p to help pay for his long journey. Jeremy

James looked across towards his Daddy, and they gave each other a cheery wave.

As Jeremy James drew closer to Santa Claus, he felt more and more excited. Santa Claus seemed such a nice man. He was talking to each of the children before he gave them their present, and he would pat them on the head and sometimes let out a jolly laugh, and only once did he seem at all un-Father-Christmas-like; that was when a little ginger-haired boy with freckles stepped up before him and said he hadn't got 50p but he wanted a present all the same. Then Father Christmas pulled a very serious face and Jeremy James distinctly heard him ask the boy if he would like a thick ear, which seemed a strange sort of present to offer. The boy wandered off grumbling, and when he was some distance away stuck his tongue out at Santa Claus, but by then the next child was on the platform and the jolly smile had returned as the hand reached out for the 50p piece.

Jeremy James noticed, with a slight twinge of disappointment, that the presents really were rather small, but as Santa Claus had had to bring so many, perhaps he simply hadn't had room for bigger ones. It was still quite exciting to look at the different shapes and the different wrappings and try to guess what was inside them, and by the time Jeremy James came face to face with the great man, his eyes were shining and his heart was thumping with anticipation.

'What's your name?' asked Santa Claus in a surprisingly young voice.

'Jeremy James,' said Jeremy James.

'And have you got 50p for Santa Claus?'

'Yes,' said Jeremy James, handing it over.

Then Santa Claus gave a big smile, and his blue eyes twinkled out from below his bushy white eyebrows, and Jeremy James could see his shining white teeth between the bushy white moustache and the bushy white beard. All the bushy whiteness looked remarkably like cotton wool, and the redness on the cheeks looked remarkably like red paint, which made Jeremy James feel that Santa Claus really was very different from everybody else he knew.

'Is it for your reindeer?' asked Jeremy James.

'What?' asked Santa Claus.

'The 50p,' said Jeremy James.

32

'Ah,' said Santa Claus, 'ah well...in a kind of a sort of a manner of speaking as you might say. Now then Jeremy James, what do you want for Christmas?'

'Oh, I'd like a tricycle, with a bell *and* a saddlebag. Gosh, is that what you're going to give me?'

'Ah no, not exactly,' said Santa Claus, 'not now anyway. Not for 50p, matey. But here's a little something to keep you going.' And Santa Claus handed him a little oblong packet wrapped in Father-Christmassy paper.

'Thank you,' said Jeremy James. 'And do you really live in the North Pole?'

'Feels like it sometimes,' said Santa Claus. 'My landlord never heats the bedrooms. Off you go. Next!'

Jeremy James carried his little packet across to where Mummy had joined Daddy to wait with the twins.

'Open it up then,' said Daddy.

Jeremy James opened it up. It was a little box. And inside the little box was a plastic car.

'Worth at least 2p,' said Daddy.

'Five,' said Jeremy James.

Jeremy James's second meeting with Santa Claus came a week and a day later. It was at a children's party in the church hall. The party began with the Reverend Cole hobbling on to the platform and saying several times in his creaky voice that he hoped everyone would enjoy himself, and the party was to end with Santa Claus coming and giving out the presents. In between, there were games, eating and drinking, and more games. As soon as the first lot of games got underway, the Reverend Cole hobbled out of the hall, and nobody even noticed that he'd gone. The games were very noisy and full of running around, and as Jeremy James was extremely good at making a noise and running around, he enjoyed himself.

The eating and drinking bit came next, and Jeremy James showed that he was just as good at eating and drinking as he was at making a noise and running around. In fact Mummy, who was one of the helpers (having left Daddy at home to mind the twins and the television set), actually stopped him when he was on the verge of breaking the world record for the number of mince pies eaten at a single go. When at last there was not a crumb left on any of the tables, the helpers cleared the empty paper plates and the empty paper cups and the not so empty wooden floor. After a few more games full of shrieks and squeaks and bumps and thumps, all the children had completely forgotten about Santa Claus, but Santa Claus had not forgotten them. At the stroke of six o'clock, one of the grown-ups called for everyone to keep quiet and stand still, and at ten past six, when everyone was quiet and standing still, the hall door opened, and in came Father Christmas.

The first thing Jeremy James noticed about Father Christmas was how slowly he walked–as if his body was very heavy and his legs very weak. He was wearing the same red coat and hood as before, and he had a white beard and moustache, but... somehow they were not nearly as bushy. His cheeks were nice and red, but... he was wearing a pair of spectacles. And when he called out to the children: 'Merry Christmas, everyone, and I hope you're enjoying yourselves!' his voice was surprisingly creaky and hollow-sounding.

Jeremy James frowned as Santa Claus heaved himself and his sack up on to the platform. There was definitely something strange about him. The other children didn't seem to notice, and they were all excited as the helpers made them line up, but perhaps the others had never met Santa Claus before, so how could they know?

Jeremy James patiently waited for his turn, and when it came, he stepped confidently up on to the platform.

'Now... er... what's your name?' said Santa Claus, peering down at Jeremy James.

'You should remember,' said Jeremy James. 'It was only a week ago that I told you.'

'Oh dear,' said Santa Claus. 'I do have a terrible memory.'

'And a week ago,' said Jeremy James, 'you weren't wearing glasses, and your voice wasn't all creaky like it is now.'

'Oh,' said Santa Claus, 'wasn't I... er... wasn't it?'

Jeremy James looked very carefully at Santa Claus's face, and Santa Claus looked back at Jeremy James with a rather puzzled expression in his... brown eyes.

'Santa Claus has blue eyes!' said Jeremy James.

'Oh!' said Santa Claus, his mouth dropping open in surprise.

'And he's got white teeth, too!' said Jeremy James.

'Hm!' said Santa Claus, closing his mouth in dismay.

34

'You're not Santa Claus at all,' said Jeremy James. 'You're not!'

And so saying, Jeremy James turned to the whole crowd of children and grown-ups, and announced at the top of his voice:

'He's a cheat! He's not Father Christmas!'

Father Christmas rose unsteadily to his feet, and as he did so, his hood fell off, revealing a shining bald head. Father Christmas hastily raised a hand to pull the hood back on, but his hand brushed against his beard and knocked it sideways, and as he tried to save his beard, he brushed against his moustache, and that fell off altogether, revealing beneath it the face of... the Reverend Cole.

'There!' said Jeremy James. 'That proves it!'

One or two of the children started crying, but then the man who had been organising the games jumped up on to the platform and explained that the real Santa Claus was very busy preparing for Christmas, and that was why the Reverend Cole had had to take his place. They hadn't wanted to disappoint the children. And it was just bad luck that there'd been such a clever little boy at the party, but the clever little boy should be congratulated all the same on being so clever, and if they could just go on pretending that the Reverend Cole was the real Santa Claus, the clever little boy should have two presents as a special reward for being so clever.

Then the Reverend Cole put on his beard and moustache and hood again, and everybody clapped very loudly as Jeremy James collected his two presents. And they were big presents, too—a book of bible stories, and a set of paints and brushes. As Jeremy James said to Mummy on the way home:

'It's funny that the real Santa Claus only gave me a rotten old car for 50p, but Mr Cole gave me these big presents for nothing.'

But as Father Christmas was a grown-up, and the Reverend Cole was also a grown-up, Jeremy James knew there was no point in trying to understand it all. Grown-ups never behave in the way you'd expect them to.

A Visit to the Bank

Shirley Jackson

Our local bank is an informal and neighbourly spot, lavish with its hard-covered cheque-books, always ready to look up the value of the Swiss franc, eager to advise on investments or make wills. I have had occasion, over the past few years, to deal frequently with the bank's Mr Andrews, a man of chilling questions and a very cynical view of me, over some minor monies which have passed reluctantly from Mr Andrews' hands into our bank account, and rapidly from there into the hands of various milkmen, doctors, department stores, and sundry poker cronies of my husband's. Mr Andrews likes to believe that he is giving me this money as a favour.

Mr Andrews never says 'money,' just like that, the way the rest of us do so often; he refers to it reverently as 'Credit' or 'Funds' or 'Equity'. I have fallen into the habit of taking one or more of my children with me when I drop in to speak to Mr Andrews about equity or funds or credit, in the unexpressed hope that their soft pathetic eyes might touch Mr Andrews' heart, although I know by now that their soft pathetic little eyes might as easily open the door to the vault.

At any rate, shortly before Christmas, then—and Christmas is of course always a time of great monetary discomfort around our house—I came timidly to Mr Andrews' bank, at the back of my mind the thought that the children's presents had at least been bought and duly hidden, although not paid for, and holding by one hand my daughter Jannie, in a blue snow-suit, and holding by the other hand my daughter Sally, in a red snow-suit. The girls had their hair brushed and their boots on the right feet, and if I could raise the cash from Mr Andrews they were each going to have an ice-cream cone. We came into the bank, where the loud-speaker system was playing 'Joy to the World', and found that the central area, where they usually foreclose mortgages, had been given over to a tall and gracious Christmas tree; because of the holiday season, they were foreclosing their mortgages in a sort of little recess behind the assistants. I sat the girls down on a velvet-covered bench directly in front of the Christmas tree, and told them to stay right where they were and mummy would be back in a minute and then we would all go and get our ice-cream cones. They sat down obediently, and I made my way over to Mr Andrews' secretary.

'Good morning,' I said to her.

'Good morning,' she said. 'Merry Christmas.'

'Oh,' I said. 'Merry Christmas.'

She nodded brightly and turned back to the papers on her desk. I twined my fingers around the ornamental ironwork of the railing, and said, 'I wonder if I might perhaps be able to see Mr Andrews?'

'Mr Andrews? And what did you want to see him about?'

'Well,' I said, coming a little closer, 'it was to have been about our loan.'

'Your loan?' she said, in that peculiarly penetrating tone all bank employees use when there is a question of money going the unnatural, or reverse-English direction. 'You wanted to pay back your loan?'

'I hoped,' I said, 'that perhaps I could speak to Mr Andrews.'

'Isn't that sweet?' she said unexpectedly.

After a minute I realized that she was staring past me to where my girls were sitting, and I turned and saw without belief that Santa Claus, complete with sack of toys, had come out from behind the Christmas tree and was leaning over the railing and beckoning my daughters to him.

'I didn't know the bank had a Santa Claus,' I said.

'Every year,' she said. 'At Christmas, you know.'

Jannie and Sally slid off the bench and trotted over to Santa Claus; I could hear Sally's delighted, 'Hello, Santa Claus!' and see Jannie's half-embarrassed smile; people all over the bank were turning to look and to beam and to smile at one another and murmur appreciatively. Because I have known Jannie and Sally for rather a long time, I untwined my fingers from the ironwork and made across the bank for their bench, reaching them just as Santa Claus opened the little gate in the railing and ushered them inside. He sat down under the warm lights of the Christmas tree and took Jannie on to one knee and Sally on to the other.

'Well, well, well,' he said, and laughed hugely. 'And have you been a *good* girl?' he asked Jannie.

Jannie nodded, her mouth open, and Sally said. 'I've been *very* good.'

'And do you brush your teeth?'

'Twice,' said Sally, and Jannie said, 'I brush *my* teeth every morning and every night and every morning.'

'Well, well, well,' Santa Claus said, nodding his head appreciatively. 'So you've been good little girls, have you?'

'I've been very *very* good,' Sally said insistently.

Santa Claus thought. 'And have you washed your faces?' was what he finally achieved.

'I wash *my* face,' said Sally, and Jannie, inspired, said 'I wash my face and my hands and my arms and my ears and my neck and–'

'Well, that's just *fine*,' Santa Claus said, and again he laughed merrily, bouncing Jannie and Sally off his round little belly. 'Fine, fine,' he said, 'and now,' he said to Jannie, 'what is old Santa going to bring you for Christmas?'

'A doll?' Jannie said tentatively. 'Are you going to bring me a doll?'

'I most certainly *am* going to bring you a doll,' said Santa Claus. 'I'm going to bring you the prettiest doll you ever *saw*, because you've been such a *good* girl.'

38

'And a wagon?' Jannie said. 'And dolls' dishes and a little stove?'

'That's *just* what I'm going to bring you,' Santa Claus said. 'I'm going to bring good little girls *every*thing they ask for.'

The fatuous smile I had been wearing on my face began to slip a little; there was a handsome doll dressed in blue waiting for Jannie in the guest-room closet, and a handsome doll dressed in pink waiting for Sally; I began trying to signal surreptitiously to Santa Claus.

'And me,' Sally said, 'and me, and *me*. I want a bicycle.'

I shook my head most violently at Santa Claus, smiling nervously. 'That's right,' Santa Claus said, 'for good little girls, I bring bicycles.'

'You're *really* going to bring me a bicycle?' Sally asked incredulously. '*And* a doll *and* a wagon?'

'I most certainly am,' Santa Claus told her.

Sally gazed raptly at Jannie. 'He's going to bring my bicycle after all,' she said.

'*I* want a bicycle too,' Jannie said.

'Alllllll right,' said Santa Claus. 'But have you been a *good* girl?' he asked Jannie anxiously.

'I've been so good,' Jannie told him with ardour, 'you just don't *know*, I've been so good.'

'I've been good,' Sally said. 'I want blocks, too. And a doll's pram for my doll, and a bicycle.'

'And our brother wants a microscope,' Jannie told Santa Claus, 'and he's been a very good boy. And a little table and chairs, I want.'

'Santa Claus,' I said, '*excuse* me, Santa Claus...'

'Aren't they darling?' a woman said behind me.

'And candy, and oranges, and nuts,' Santa Claus was going on blissfully, 'and all sorts of good things in your stockings, and candy canes—'

'I forgot, I want a party dress.'

'But you must be *good* little girls, and do just what your mummy and daddy tell you to, and never, *never* forget to brush your teeth.'

I went with haste back to Mr Andrews' secretary. 'I've *got* to see Mr Andrews,' I told her, 'I've got to see him *fast*.'

'You'll have to wait,' she said, looking fondly over to where my daughters were receiving a final pat on the head from Santa Claus.

The loud-speaker system was playing 'O Come, All Ye Faithful', I was thinking wildly: bicycle, microscope, bicycle, table and chairs, dolls' dishes, and my daughters came running across the floor to me. 'Look,' Sally was shrieking, 'look at what Santa Claus gave to us.'

'Santa Claus was here,' Jannie confirmed, 'he came right into the bank where we were and he gave us each a present, look, a little bag of chocolate money.'

'Oh, fine, fine, fine,' I said madly.

'And I *am* going to have my bicycle, Santa said he was *too* bringing it.'

'—and me a bicycle too, and a doll's pram and dishes and—'

'—and in our stockings.'

'Mr Andrews will see you now,' said the secretary.

I sat my daughters down again and made my entrance into Mr Andrews' office. His nose still retained a trace of jovial redness, but the jolly old elf's eye was the familiar agate, and the faint echo of jingle bells around him sounded more like the clinking of half dollars.

'Well,' said Santa Claus, selecting my loan slip from the stack on his desk, 'and what brings *you* here again so soon?'

Burper and the Magic Lamp

Robert Leeson

This is the story of Roderick. That is what his parents called him. Don't ask me why. Parents do funny things when they choose names for their children.

But in class, they call him Burper.

Not to his face of course. Oh no.

They called him Burper for a very good reason. He was always burping. He didn't do it after school dinner, like anybody might—just once at the beginning of the afternoon. He would do it at break time. He would do it in PE. He'd do it in English. He'd even do it in Assembly.

Miss would look up, over her glasses and say, 'Which ill-mannered person did that?'

Everybody knew who'd done it. But they didn't say. Not on your nelly. Miss probably knew, but she couldn't be sure. After all if someone has just burped how can you prove it? Do you take a tape recording and hold an identity parade?

So Roderick got away with it. He got away with most things. He was bigger than anyone in the class. He was bigger than anyone in the school. Whichever way you looked at him he was bigger. He was bigger this way and he was bigger that way.

Now some people get fat because they are unhappy and some people get fat because there's something wrong with their body.

There were two things wrong with Burper. He ate too much and he didn't get any exercise. His parents thought he was marvellous and they waited on him at home. And people waited on him at school. He made them. Anything Burper had to do, someone else did it for him. And to be honest, Burper was a pig. A big, fat, pig.

He always got his way. He always got what he wanted. And the more he got, the more he wanted.

But what he wanted most of all, he couldn't have.

Poor old Burper.

Well, not really.

What happened was that Burper fell in love.

It was a disaster.

He fell disastrously in love.

A new girl came to our school. She was called Djamila. She was very small. She was the smallest in the class. She had dark brown eyes with long eyelashes and wore her hair in two plaits down her back.

When she started in the class everyone held their breath.

They all knew what was going to happen. That big onk Burper was going to go up behind her and pull those plaits. Or maybe he was going to tie them together. Or tie her to the railings in the school yard by them. It wasn't fair. Burper was the biggest in the class, but he always picked on the smallest. Funny, isn't it?

Some of the lads and some of the girls wondered what they should do about it. Djamila was so small and thin, it seemed rotten to let Godzilla (or rather Burper) get his paws on her. The trouble was though, not what you *should* do about it, but what you *could* do about it.

The first day Djamila came to school it was raining. No one could go out in the yard. Miss was out of the classroom somewhere. Suddenly there was Burper creeping up behind Djamila. He was actually creeping. Imagine an elephant on tip toe. That was it.

Everyone held their breath and waited.

Just as Burper got a foot away from Djamila, she turned round so quickly, one of her plaits hit him in the eye. He jumped like a scalded cat (a scalded elephant) and Djamila said, 'Hello fat boy. What's your name?'

She said it so sweetly that Burper didn't know what to do with himself. He stuttered. He actually stuttered.

From the back of the class someone whispered (loud enough for her to hear, but not loud enough for him to tell who had spoken).

'His name's Burper.'

'Oh,' said Djamila. 'Is that your first name or your second name.'

Burper burst out, 'Roderick.'

'Oh, is that Roderick Burper or Burper Roderick? I'm not used to which way round names go.'

The whole class began to laugh.

She went on. Some people thought she was putting Burper on. But she wasn't. Her face was quite straight.

'Can I call you Burper?'

The class howled and the place was in an uproar when in walked Miss.

'Ha hm,' she said in that way of hers. 'Do you mind?'

The class went quiet. Miss looked at Burper and pointed to his seat. Burper went quietly.

Miss said, 'Djamila is starting with us today. I hope you'll all be friends with her.'

Djamila put her hand up.

'I've made one friend already, Miss. Burper.'

People all round the class started to choke. Miss tried to keep a straight face.

'Strictly speaking, Djamila, he is called Roderick.'

'Oh,' Djamila looked a bit confused now. 'I thought friends called him Burper.'

The class looked round at Burper to see how he was taking it. But it was weird. He wasn't screwing his face up like he does when he's deciding whether to twist somebody's arm off, or pull their hair till their eyes water. He sat there with a great, daft smile on his face.

43

It took Miss at least ten minutes to get the class settled down. Everybody knew, though, that something rather special had happened. They didn't know it was only just starting.

That lunchtime two lads who chanced their arm and called Roderick Burper just for fun, got minced. That hadn't changed. But the same day, when school finished, Djamila walked out of class and waved to him and called, 'See you tomorrow, Burper.'

And he went all mushy and said, 'Err-gghhh.'

Next day, and all the week, and all the next week, Burper could be seen hanging around Djamila. She had lots of friends, pretty quickly. She was that sort of girl. And after that first day, of course, she was a kind of heroine. But after the first few days, she didn't really pay much attention to Burper. The fact was, Burper wasn't really brilliant as company. His conversation was a bit limited. It was 'Gimme that,' or 'I'll thump you,' or 'You wait till break.'

And that didn't go down with Djamila. But he would hang about with her crowd, sometimes standing behind her. He wasn't planning to tie her plaits together either. He just stood there and breathed.

Sometimes she'd turn round and say, 'Hello, Burper.'

And he would answer, 'Errgghh.'

Or sometimes she would say, when he was breathing more heavily than usual, 'Please don't do that, Burper. You're giving me goose pimples.'

And then one day, when he was standing too close, she even lost her patience with him and said, 'Do leave it, Burper.'

The crowd round waited for Burper to fly into a rage. But he didn't, he just looked like an elephant whose bun ration has been stopped, and crawled back to his seat. That lunch-time he thought some of the lads were laughing at him (he was right). So he duffed them up, and felt a bit better. But towards the end of the afternoon he started looking miserable again.

'Is there something wrong, Roderick?' asked Miss. 'Perhaps you'd better go and see nurse.'

The class started laughing. But outside in the yard, nobody got clobbered. Burper just went slowly and sadly home.

It was just about then that the class started to make plans for the Christmas show. Since they were top class, they got to put on the Christmas Play. And Miss had a smashing idea. She came into class one morning with a parcel which she unwrapped.

She held up an old metal thing, a bit like an old boot with a curly end.

'Can anyone guess what this is?' she asked.

'Do you really want us to, Miss?' asked one very witty chap at the back.

'I want you to be sensible,' said Miss raising her eyebrows.

Then Djamila spoke.

'It's an old lamp, Miss. Like people used to use sometime at home, in days gone by. You put oil in it, and there's a little light at the end.'

'I thought you'd recognize it, Djamila. Right. It's an old lamp. My uncle brought it home from Baghdad. And guess what play we're going to put on.'

'Let's get lit up,' suggested someone.

'This is a serious question,' said Miss in her 'that's enough' voice.

'*Aladdin*,' shouted several. And of course it was. And no one was surprised when she chose Djamila to be the Princess. It was obvious.

'Now, we have to choose Aladdin.'

Before anyone could move, Burper had his hand up. So one or

45

two other lads who had thought of volunteering suddenly changed their minds. Miss kept a straight face, but slowly shook her head.

'Roderick. No. I'm afraid you do not look the part.'

She said it in a kindly way. But everybody knew what she meant. So did he.

Some smart alec at the back whispered, 'How about Widow Twankie? He'd look great in drag.'

There was a hush. But Burper didn't even turn round. At the end of the day, he was seen arguing with Miss by her desk. And she was shaking her head. He was getting desperate. But she would not give in. And Miss was one person in the class he couldn't lean on (apart from Djamila, that is).

Next morning there was a bit of a panic. Miss had discovered the lamp was missing. The most important prop for the Panto had gone. There was a big to-do. In the end Miss said, 'If that lamp is not back on my desk by tomorrow morning, then no Panto. And the whole school will know—and your parents—why there's no Panto.'

One or two (well about twenty-five to be exact) were pretty sure who had nicked the old lamp. Yes, no prizes. It was Burper. He'd had away with it and hidden it round the back where the dustbins are. He couldn't make up his mind what to do with it. He was better at thumping than thinking. Should he stick it right down inside one of the bins, then the rubbish van would take it away and that would fix the Panto for good and all? Or should he 'find' it and make himself the hero of the day—and perhaps the hero of the panto? But Burper wasn't so stupid. He had his doubts about what Miss would do. She might blame him for taking it. And that wouldn't be fair, would it?

So that break-time it was raining again. While the class was indoors, Burper sneaked out to the toilets. Or he pretended to and went round to the rubbish bins instead. There were four of them, about six foot high, and he could hide behind them. He found the lamp where he had put it under one of the hoppers and held it up. It was covered in dirt though. He couldn't take it back like that could he? Without thinking he rubbed it on his sleeve.

Ka-bang.

Right in front of him was a bloke. A huge bloke. He made Burper look like Peter Pan. He was as big as a door, broad and

dressed like Ali Baba. His hands were folded and he had a deep, deep voice.

'What is thy will, O Master?'

Burper, who had been crouching down, sat back in a puddle.

'Blimey,' he said. He was overcome.

'I am the slave of the lamp. Whatever you wish shall be yours.'

Burper recovered his wits.

'Hey, mister. I want to be Aladdin in the Pantomime.'

The genie shook his head.

'I do not understand. Alah-el-Din is no longer in the land of the living. He has been taken into Paradise.'

Burper bit his lip. This was going to be dodgy. Then he had a brainwave.

He pointed to himself and said, 'I, Roderick, am too fat.'

The genie looked him over, smiled and said, 'That is right. Ho-Ho.'

Burper didn't like that, but time was slipping away.

'I-want-to-lose-weight,' he said slowly.

A look of understanding came onto the genie's face. 'Aha. Lose weight.'

The genie waved his hand, and vanished into the lamp.

Burper looked at himself. And waited. And looked at himself again. There was no difference. He bent down and picked up the lamp. Either this thing didn't work or the genie had got it wrong.

But as he bent down, the ground seemed to go farther away from him. No, it wasn't the ground which was going farther away. He was going farther away from the ground. He was rising up in the air. His feet were off the ground. He struggled and kicked out with his legs, but it made no difference. He was up as high as the top of the hoppers now, and his struggles didn't bring him down to earth. They just made him move along six feet off the ground. He was like a balloon, light as a feather. Slowly it came into his brain what had happened.

He'd 'lost weight'. But he hadn't got any thinner. He was sailing along now. The rain had stopped and there was a slight breeze. Like a plump airship he was gliding towards the school. He was going to go 'splat' on the wall.

In a panic he used his right leg like a rudder. At the last moment he changed course and hung there just outside the window. Inside the class there was pandemonium as they saw Burper suspended in mid-air outside the glass, holding the lamp in front of him.

'It's a plane,' they shouted. 'No, it's a bird.' 'No.' They all groaned. 'It's Burper.'

Miss wasn't standing any nonsense. She marched to the window. She threw it open.

'Come inside and sit down, Roderick. Immediately.'

The breeze wafted Burper in across the classroom. His head went clonk on the opposite wall. Two of the lads helpfully reached up with their rulers and pushed him off. Away he went across the space between floor and ceiling.

'Shut the window,' ordered Miss quickly. The window was shut just as Burper tapped against it. Miss marched out from her desk again and got hold of Burper's wind-cheater and dragged him back down to his place. She got him sat down—which took some pushing and pulling, but no sooner had she stepped back and said, 'Now Roderick, just what do you think you are playing at?' When up he popped again and started spinning slowly round. Every time Miss tried to grasp him, he spun away again. He was getting so dizzy he couldn't see straight. Now several lads and girls joined in, trying to help. At least that's what they reckoned they were doing. But in fact it only made matters worse. It was like a gigantic balloon game. Before long the classroom was in chaos with everyone joining in. It was more fun than sports day, more fun than the Christmas Party, more fun than the time the tents came down at the school camp. It was hilarious. It was a riot.

It might have gone on for ever, well, till lunch time at least, but then something quite unexpected happened.

Djamila stood up and called, 'Burper.'

Burper stopped whirling round in the air and looked down.

'Drop the lamp!'

He dropped the lamp and Djamila caught it neatly.

While everyone watched open-mouthed, she raised the lamp in the air and spoke very clearly and slowly in another language.

There was a whistling sound and a terrific crash as Burper dropped like a stone on top of a desk. It bent, but it didn't break, fortunately. Miss helped Burper up on to his feet and took him out to Nurse to get his bumps seen to. In all the noise and confusion no one noticed, until Miss came back, that Djamila had gone.

Next day, the class heard that her family had moved away. Everyone was sorry, because life was just that little bit slower and duller now Djamila wasn't there.

No one was more sorry than Burper. For weeks he didn't talk to anyone. Not even 'Gimme that,' or 'I'll thump you.' He never explained how he'd come to be floating like a balloon across the classroom that day. And Miss decided there was no point in trying to find out.

The old lamp had gone, too, so that rather scrubbed round Aladdin for the Christmas Play. Miss had to think of something, fairly quickly, so people could choose the parts and start rehearsing.

Burper wasn't seen in the dining hall for weeks. He was spotted lurking round the school yard with a packet of crispbread and a tomato. And once or twice, lads and girls who had newspaper rounds spotted him jogging round the park, puffing away to himself.

Miss chose *Cinderella*. Burper, who had lost two stone, got the part of Buttons. You wouldn't chuckle! But he didn't seem to mind. He did it rather well.

He's stopped thumping people—well no more than average, anyway. He's stopped burping in class. But that's the trouble with nicknames. This one's stuck to him.

But he's in better condition now. And anyone who calls him Burper to his face had better have twenty yards start.

Brown Baby

Gwen Grant

My Gran says if she'd ever been asked to be an angel, which she hasn't, not once, not ever, and that is sixty odd years she was talking about, well...

'Tha'll be asked to be an angel soon enough,' my Grandad puts in. 'And tha'll not be able to refuse,' and my Gran snorts and says what does he know about anything, ay? And he says one thing he does know about is angels.

'For instance?' says my Grandma.

'For instance,' says Grandad. 'Angels has to have costumes, that's a for instance. They don't walk about with nothing on, you know.'

My Gran sniffs and tells my Grandad that if he *must* talk Dirty, he'd be better employed washing his mouth out with soap and water than stuffing it full of disgusting pipe smoke.

Our Kevin rolls over and over on the rug, clutching his stomach and shouting, 'They walk about BARE, do angels. Bare bottoms. Bare bottoms.' So then Gran has to haul him onto his feet and say, 'There'll be no sweets for you, my lad, if you don't shut up.'

Kevin grins at my Grandad and Grandad winks at him and before we can talk about a costume for this Angel Gabriel, which is what I am going to be in the Christmas play at school, Mr Kumumba comes to the door and knocks on it three times.

'Ask that lad to come in,' my Grandad tells Kevin but Kevin shakes his head and says 'No,' and then hides behind my Grandma's apron.

'Come in, Oti,' Grandma shouts and Mr K. stalks in with a great big grin on his face.

'She's all right,' he says, and my Gran gets all excited and shouts 'Has she had the baby, then?' And Mr Kumumba says she has and what's more, it's a boy.

'A Christmas baby,' my Gran gloats, and Grandad gets out of

his chair and fetches a bottle of beer for him and Mr Kumumba, which they drink straight off.

'So, Patricia. A brother for you,' Mr Kumumba says, and I nod because—this is the thing—this person who has had this baby is mine and Kevin's Mum, who is called Marion.

'I want my Dad,' our Kevin yells but he can't have him on account of how our Dad is living in Australia.

'Let me be your Dad, Kevin,' Mr Kumumba says slowly and holds out a hand to Kevin, which our Kevin straightaway bites.

Well, that's one way to make a happy Christmas, I must say. My Gran is going to give Kev a walloping but Mr Kumumba just says 'Leave the child alone. We'll have to work on this,' and Gran settles for glaring at our Kev till he bursts into tears.

Then she cuddles him up and he hits out at her and yells, 'Let go of me, you. I want my Dad,' and that's it for nineteen hours because once he starts, there's no stopping him.

Two days later, our Mam comes home from hospital and she brings this little brown baby with her and she and Mr Kumumba dress it in a blue romper suit and a hat with pom-poms on it.

'I hope you're going to love the new baby, Patricia,' my Mam says and I look at this baby and it doesn't look all that great, if you ask me.

'We're not asking you,' Marion says firmly and then says I must not call her Marion and can't I have a bash at calling Mr Kumumba by his first name if I can't bring myself to call him Dad?

'No, Marion,' I says. 'You and Mr Kumumba aren't our Mam and Dad,' and Kev picks up his little spade and goes outside to play miners.

It seems a bit daft to me asking us to call Mr K. 'Dad'. He's very black and we're not. Neither of us. Neither me and our Kevin nor Marion are black and neither is this new baby either. He's brown.

'Tha'll be able to make your own rainbow, you lot,' Shawn Parker shouts at me, so I kick his teeth in, which is an accident as I didn't think I'd be able to kick that hard. I am very glad I am mistaken.

Bong, bong, bong, Shawn P. goes on my head with his fist.

'Here's the blue,' he snarls.

Scrawk, scratch, I go.

'And there's the red,' I snarl back, as all Shawn P.'s blood starts

51

to drip down his skin, and then after that, my Gran pulls us apart and Mrs Parker tells her that she ought to take us back where we came from (the jungle), and that's just about what happens most days since mine and Kevin's Mam married Mr Kumumba.

''ave you seen what *he's* doing?' Mrs Parker asks our Gran and Gran shakes her head and says, 'I don't care what *he's* doing. All I care about is that you mind your own business.'

'Very well,' shouts Mrs P. 'Then you'll not care that he's burying that new baby.'

I have to hand it to my Gran. She just walks until she is out of Mrs Parker's sight and then she goes down the passage like a two-year old.

'What you doing, Kevin?' she yells in a whisper and there's Kevin, a hole the size of an upside-down Everest in the garden, and the new brown baby who was lying a minute ago in his snuggle-hood and coat in his pram, only now he's under six ton of soil.

'Dear heavens,' my Gran screams aloud, so it must be a real emergency, given that Mrs Parker is leaning over her fence two doors down and can hear anything above a whisper. 'What have you done, child? What have you done?'

'Shall I send for an ambulance?' Mrs Parker shouts and Shawn Parker says 'More like the men in white coats,' so Mrs P. swipes him one and tells him to keep his mouth shut while she's talking.

My Grandad says it would be a better idea if Mrs Parker kept her mouth shut, full stop.

'Screech,' goes Mrs P. and disappears.

Gran fishes the new brown baby out of the pram and it's coughing and spluttering like a little kitten.

Snit, snit, it goes and that's supposed to be a sneeze.

'Whew,' my Gran breathes and holds the baby very close to her and then she starts to cry. 'Kevin, Kevin,' she sobs and the new baby suddenly howls. He sounds like a rock group.

Gran brushes all this dirt off him and keeps saying, 'Cry, little lad, cry. Clear those lungs,' and the little lad certainly does that. He has to have the clearest lungs in town. I think he'll never shut up.

'You bad lad, Kevin,' my Gran says and Kev, who is six years old and old enough to know better, my Grandad says, he starts crying as well.

Marion and Mr Kumumba aren't very happy, I can tell you, to find the brown baby has almost turned into an angel before his time.

Mr Kumumba sits in the stuffed chair in the corner of the front room and he looks like a worried Snoopy.

'It'll be all right, Mr K.,' I tells him and he looks up at me and says 'Thank you, Patricia,' and for the first time, I start to think there may be more to this fellow than meets the eye.

I almost decide to call Marion 'Mam' again but decide not to rush into anything.

'Erm, about this here Angel, Gran.' I finally brings the talk round to my Angel Gabriel costume, which was where we started, and Gran says she's got a nice sheet, the wings will be no problem, and Grandad can make a halo in his sleep.

Kev stops yelling and stares at Grandad.

'He,' I tell them, pointing to Kevin, 'he's going to be Joseph.'

'What?' says Marion. 'That's the first I've heard of it.'

'There's somebody from every class in this play,' I tell them. 'And our Kev is Joseph and he needs a costume as well.'

My Grandad says he has a very old brown potato sack that will be just the thing for Joseph and Mr Kumumba says he has an original head-dress that Joseph himself would probably have worn.

'The real thing, Kevin,' he says gravely. 'Beautiful square of white cloth and the black twisted band that goes around the head,' and he says it in his dark voice.

Kevin stares at the carpet and keeps quiet, stupid kid.

So, we gets all set up and starts going to rehearsals at school in the afternoons, which isn't bad because it gets you out of some work, but which is bad because I find out that Shawn Parker is the Innkeeper.

'That kid of yourn won't get his little toe into shelter,' he says, and pummels our Kevin's head further down his neck.

'Leave him alone,' I warn him but he laughs and shouts 'What's a stupid lass like you gonna do about it, if I don't?' But luckily I don't need to do anything as Kev tries to take a chunk out of Parker's left leg with his teeth.

'Let go of him,' I order our Kev. 'You'll get food poisoning.' And that doesn't have Parker smiling, I can tell you.

Miss Twistle, who is the teacher in charge of the concert, she announces, 'There will be one last rehearsal, children. Tomorrow afternoon and then... ah, then, the real thing tomorrow night,' and she flutters her eyelashes and looks up at the ceiling.

I look up as well because I half expect to see Angel Gabriel lounging on the plaster and keeping an eye on things but if he is, he is keeping it very quiet.

We have a very good run-through in the afternoon rehearsal. Miss Twistle brings in a real live doll called Tiny Tears which cries, wets its nappy, and takes a bottle.

'Can it be sick?' asks our Kevin, and Shawn Parker laughs coarsely and says 'It makes me sick and that's a fact,' and then he stamps on my toe and goes on, 'And so do you.'

Miss Twistle says her own stomach does not remain unmoved, 'when I see your unlovely countenance, Parker.'

Shawn Parker scowls and says he is looking forward to the play.

'See me?' he says to Mary, who is five and a half and happens to be a Pakistani, 'See me?' and Mary nods. 'Well,' prod prod goes Parker with his finger on her shoulder, 'you're not getting in to no shelter. Hah!' he roars. 'Tha can stop out in the cold and FREEZE.'

Mary's eyes start to fill up with tears, so Parker rushes on, 'To death, see. Yer can freeze to death,' and then Mary starts crying all over Tiny Tears and Miss Twistle snaps, 'Beyond human endurance, Parker,' and lands him one sharply on the knuckles.

This brings that rehearsal to a close and then, before we know where we are, it's time for the REAL THING.

'Have you got your costumes?' Marion asks and when we both nod our heads and say 'Yes, Marion,' she says that if there are any angels, which she personally doubts, she'd be very much obliged if they would take a hand in things and remind us she was called 'MOTHER,' she roars.

That leaves me and our Kevin unmoved, I can tell you, especially since brown baby is screaming at the top of his voice.

'Nicholas!' Marion roars again. 'Not brown baby. His name is Nicholas.'

'Oh, very festive,' Miss Twistle says when she meets Marion, Mr Kumumba, and brown baby at the school. 'A lovely name,' and starts looking pale because brown baby is still yelling at the top of his voice.

'He'll settle down,' Marion tells her.

Mr Kumumba says how much he's looking forward to the concert and Miss Twistle nods to Mrs Parker and Mr Parker and then all us actors go behind the stage to get ready.

Everything goes smashing. Really smashing, not just ordinary smashing–until it is time for the baby Jesus to appear.

'Where's Tiny Tears?' Miss Twistle starts screaming quietly.

Everybody looks for Tiny Tears but nobody can find her. She's gone.

'Well, we've got to have a baby Jesus,' Miss Twistle says, chewing the edges of her handkerchief.

The school choir are just finishing 'Away in a manger' and then the lights go down ready for the main spotlight to go on Mary, Joseph, and baby Jesus and it does and there is nobody there.

Quiver, goes the spotlight, and starts looking around the stage for them.

'Hum,' Miss Twistle orders the choir. 'Hum,' and they start humming but they all pick a different tune, so Mrs Savage on the piano, she starts playing 'Away in a Manger' again and that gets the choir going.

'No baby,' Miss Twistle's going and then she rockets through to the audience and Bingo, she's back with brown baby in her arms.

'We're very lucky,' she sobs. 'Mrs Kumumba has lent us Nicholas,' and Kevin goes stark eyed when he sees brown baby in his concert. 'What we'll do,' Miss Twistle says, 'is to sit Mary down with Nicholas on her knees and on no account, Mary,' Miss Twistle says firmly, 'are you to move an inch.'

All at once I start getting worried about brown baby and I tell young Mary that one wrong move on her part and zip... Mary looks at me all worried... 'Zip,' I repeat. 'Your head will roll.'

Mary covers her face and starts yelling she doesn't want to be Mary any more but Miss Twistle just shows her brown baby's face and she decides she does, after all.

The stage goes black again and Mary, Joseph, Miss Twistle, and brown baby creep on from one side while Shawn Parker goes on the other.

Up goes the spotlight and there's Mary with brown baby on her knee and Joseph banging on the door of the inn.

'Waddjawant?' snarls the Innkeeper when he answers the door, and you could cover Shawn Parker in a tin of paint and a double bed you'd still know it was him the minute he opens his mouth.

'We want a bed for the night,' squeaks Joseph.

'A wot?' growls Innkeeper.

'A bed,' says young Kev. 'For me and Mary and brow... baby Jesus.'

'Tha's not getting one,' Innkeeper roars. Mary bursts into tears and brown baby blows bubbles.

Joseph's eyes get as big as buckets as he sees this Innkeeper towering over him.

'Wot's more,' shouts Shawn Parker, 'tha can tek thi babby and get lost,' and he starts to march towards Mary and brown baby.

'We want a bed,' Joseph says and his voice is shaking. 'Just for the night, Mister. To keep baby Jesus out of the snow,' he squeaks and by the time he's finished talking, his voice is somewhere up around the top of the school roof.

'Gggggggrrrrrowwwwwwwwwwlllll,' goes Innkeeper and reaches down to touch brown baby.

Hop, goes Joseph and before anyone can blink, has brown baby in his arms. Well, half in his arms and half on Mary's lap.

'Leave the baby alone,' he yells. 'Leave Jesus alone,' and with his teeth, which don't happen to be doing anything right then, he takes a bite out of Innkeeper's arm.

'Scream,' goes Parker and then stutters, 'Ah, yer can sleep in the manger, if tha wants,' and wild-eyed Kevin, he stands clutching the top half of brown baby as if there's no tomorrow, while Mary's hanging on to the bottom. The smelly bit.

'Come,' roars Joseph. 'We will go to the manger,' and then the lights go out, Miss Twistle erupts onto the stage, and rescues Nicholas.

'Very good,' she says to Joseph and pats Mary. I daresay if she'd had a hammer in her hand, she'd have patted Innkeeper as well but as she doesn't she just says, 'Quite got into the part there, Parker, didn't you?'

Well, that is it.

Kev doesn't mind brown baby any more. I don't mind him either and we both call Marion 'Mam' again.

Mr Kumumba takes us to his mother's for Christmas but boy, that is a whole new ball game!

Yeah, man!

Carol-barking

Laurie Lee

Towards Christmas there was heavy snow, which raised the roads to the top of the hedges. There were millions of tons of the lovely stuff, plastic, pure, all-purpose, which nobody owned, which one could carve or tunnel, eat, or just throw about. It covered the hills and cut off the villages, but nobody thought of rescues; for there was hay in the barns and flour in the kitchens, the women baked bread, the cattle were fed and sheltered—we'd been cut off before, after all.

The week before Christmas, when snow seemed to lie thickest, was the moment for carol-singing; and when I think back to those nights it is to the crunch of snow and to the lights of the lanterns on it. Carol-singing in my village was a special tithe for the boys, the girls had little to do with it. Like hay-making, black-berrying, stone-clearing and wishing-people-a-happy-Easter, it was one of our seasonal perks.

By instinct we knew just when to begin it; a day too soon and we should have been unwelcome, a day too late and we should have received lean looks from people whose bounty was already exhausted. When the true moment came, exactly balanced, we recognized it and were ready.

So as soon as the wood had been stacked in the oven to dry for the morning fire, we put on our scarves and went out through the streets, calling loudly between our hands, till the various boys who knew the signal ran out from their houses to join us.

One by one they came stumbling over the snow, swinging their lanterns around their heads, shouting and coughing horribly.

'Coming carol-barking then?'

We were the Church Choir, so no answer was necessary. For a year we had praised the Lord out of key, and as a reward for this service—on top of the Outing—we now had the right to visit all the big houses, to sing our carols and collect our tribute.

To work them all in meant a five-mile foot journey over wild and generally snowed-up country. So the first thing we did was to plan our route; a formality, as the route never changed. All the same, we blew on our fingers and argued; and then we chose our Leader. This was not binding, for we all fancied ourselves as Leaders, and he who started the night in that position usually trailed home with a bloody nose.

Eight of us set out that night. There was Sixpence the Simple, who had never sung in his life (he just worked his mouth in Church); the brothers Horace and Boney, who were always fighting everybody and always getting the worst of it; Clergy Green, the preaching maniac; Walt the bully, and my two brothers. As we went down the lane other boys, from other villages, were already about the hills, bawling 'Kingwenslush', and shouting through keyholes 'Knock on the knocker! Ring at the Bell! Give us a penny for singing so well!' They weren't an approved charity as we were, the Choir; but competition was in the air.

Our first call as usual was the house of the Squire, and we trooped nervously down his drive. For light we had candles in marmalade-jars suspended on loops of string, and they threw pale gleams on the towering snowdrifts that stood on each side of the drive. A blizzard was blowing, but we were well wrapped up, with Army puttees on our legs, woollen hats on our heads, and several scarves around our ears.

As we approached the Big House across its white silent lawns, we too grew respectfully silent. The lake nearby was stiff and black, the waterfall frozen and still. We arranged ourselves shuffling around the big front door, then knocked and announced the Choir.

A maid bore the tidings of our arrival away into the echoing distances of the house, and while we waited we cleared our throats noisily. Then she came back, and the door was left ajar for us, and we were bidden to begin. We brought no music, the carols were in our heads. 'Let's give 'em "Wild Shepherds",' said Jack. We began in confusion, plunging into a wreckage of keys, of different words and tempo; but we gathered our strength; he who sang loudest took the rest of us with him, and the carol took shape if not sweetness.

This huge stone house, with its ivied walls, was always a

mystery to us. What were those gables, those rooms and attics, those narrow windows veiled by the cedar trees? As we sang 'Wild Shepherds' we craned our necks, gaping into that lamplit hall which we had never entered; staring at the muskets and untenanted chairs, the great tapestries furred by dust—until suddenly, on the stairs, we saw the old Squire himself standing and listening with his head on one side.

He didn't move until we'd finished; then slowly he tottered towards us, dropped two coins in our box with a trembling hand, scratched his name in the book we carried, gave us each a long look with his moist blind eyes, then turned away in silence.

As though released from a spell, we took a few sedate steps, then broke into a run for the gate. We didn't stop till we were out of the grounds. Impatient, at last, to discover the extent of his bounty, we squatted by the cowsheds, held our lanterns over the book, and saw that he had written 'Two Shillings'. This was quite a good start. No one of any worth in the district would dare to give us less than the Squire.

So with money in the box, we pushed on up the valley, pouring scorn on each other's performance. Confident now, we began to consider our quality and whether one carol was not better suited to us than another. Horace, Walt said, shouldn't sing at all; his voice was beginning to break. Horace disputed this and there was a brief token battle—they fought as they walked, kicking up divots of snow, then they forgot it, and Horace still sang.

Steadily we worked through the length of the valley, going from house to house, visiting the lesser and the greater gentry—the farmers, the doctors, the merchants, the majors and other exalted persons. It was freezing hard and blowing too; yet not for a moment did we feel the cold. The snow blew into our faces, into our eyes and mouths, soaked through our puttees, got into our boots, and dripped from our woollen caps. But we did not care. The collecting-box grew heavier, and the list of names in the book longer and more extravagant, each trying to outdo the other.

Mile after mile we went, fighting against the wind, falling into snowdrifts, and navigating by the lights of the houses. And yet we never saw our audience. We called at house after house; we sang in courtyards and porches, outside windows, or in the damp gloom of hallways; we heard voices from hidden rooms; we smelt rich clothes and strange hot food; we saw maids bearing in dishes or

60

carrying away coffee-cups; we received nuts, cakes, figs, preserved ginger, dates, cough-drops and money; but we never once saw our patrons. We sang as it were at the castle walls, and apart from the Squire, who had shown himself to prove that he was still alive, we never expected it otherwise.

As the night drew on there was trouble with Boney. 'Noël', for instance, had a rousing harmony which Boney persisted in singing, and singing flat. The others forbade him to sing it at all, and Boney said he would fight us. Picking himself up, he agreed we were right, then he disappeared altogether. He just turned away and walked into the snow and wouldn't answer when we called him back. Much later, as we reached a far point up the valley, somebody said 'Hark!' and we stopped to listen. Far away across the fields from the distant village came the sound of a frail voice singing, singing 'Noël', and singing it flat–it was Boney, branching out on his own.

We approached our last house high up on the hill, the place of Joseph the farmer. For him we had chosen a special carol, which was about the other Joseph, so that we always felt that singing it added a spicy cheek to the night. The last stretch of country to reach his farm was perhaps the most difficult of all. In these rough bare lanes, open to all winds, sheep were buried and wagons lost. Huddled together, we tramped in one another's footsteps, powdered snow blew into our screwed-up eyes, the candles burnt low, some blew out altogether, and we talked loudly above the gale.

Crossing, at last, the frozen mill-stream–whose wheel in summer still turned a barren mechanism–we climbed up to Joseph's farm. Sheltered by trees, warm on its bed of snow, it seemed always to be like this. As always it was late; as always this was our final call. The snow had a fine crust upon it, and the old trees sparkled like tinsel.

We grouped ourselves round the farmhouse porch. The sky cleared, and broad streams of stars ran down over the valley and away to Wales. On Slad's white slopes, seen through the black sticks of its woods, some red lamps still burned in the windows.

Everything was quiet; everywhere there was the faint crackling silence of the winter night. We started singing, and we were all moved by the words and the sudden trueness of our voices. Pure, very clear, and breathless we sang:

As Joseph was a walking
He heard an angel sing;
'This night shall be the birth-time
Of Christ the Heavenly King.

He neither shall be bornèd
In Housen nor in hall,
Nor in a place of paradise
But in an ox's stall . . . .'

And 2,000 Christmasses became real to us then; the houses, the halls, the places of paradise had all been visited; the stars were bright to guide the Kings through the snow; and across the farmyard we could hear the beasts in their stalls. We were given roast apples and hot mince-pies, in our nostrils were spices like myrrh, and in our wooden box, as we headed back for the village, there were golden gifts for all.

Welcome, Yule

Jan Mark

Probably Emma would not have come to know Mr Jarvis, the new vicar, if someone had not tipped him off that her dad could play the organ. They never discovered who had done it, although Dad did say that whoever it was ought to be hung up by the heels and skinned with a butter knife, which would have been worth watching, but one day the vicar arrived on his motor cycle, without warning. Emma came home from school and found him in the living room with a cup of tea at his elbow, Mum hovering and Dad cowering.

'I believe you're something of an organist,' said the vicar, to Emma's dad, who was off work with a broken finger. He was a draughtsman at Featherstone's.

'Not at the moment,' Dad said, waving his fat finger like a parsnip in its bandages.

'Well, that won't last forever,' the vicar said.

'Nor will I,' Dad said, glumly. He hated to be ill, even in one finger. Emma loved it because she was healthy and hardly ever had a day off school.

'It would only be two weeks in three,' said Mr Jarvis. 'There's no music at Holy Communion.' He would not give in. After about an hour, Dad gave in, because his finger would keep him off the keys for at least another month and, as the vicar had said, it was only two Sundays out of three.

Ockney, Cawley and Strang shared one vicar among them. Emma lived in Strang, and the vicar did too, because it was the largest parish. It had a council estate, a factory, and the smallest Woolworth's in England, perhaps in the whole world. On Sundays he buzzed in a beeline from church to church on his motor cycle; Holy Communion at Ockney, Matins at Strang and Evensong at Cawley. On the following Sunday they each celebrated a different service. Emma thought it was like musical

64

chairs, and wondered what would happen if one of the churches fell down during the week, and the vicar was left stranded with a spare service and nowhere to say it. Churches had fallen down before. On the hill above Strang, between Highmead Estate and Featherstone's Marine Diesel Engines Ltd, lay the remains of St Thomas's church. Six hundred years ago old Strang village had stood on the hill around St Thomas's, but after the Black Death, which wiped out all but seven parishioners, the village moved away and started again in the valley, with a new church, Holy Trinity, which showed no signs of falling down.

Up on the hill, St Thomas's slid gently back into the ground until the grass covered it, and now the local children played on the green lumps and bumps that had been the nave and chancel. They preferred it to the council playground where there were swings and slides and concrete pipes to crawl through. Emma herself preferred it. She did not live on the council estate, but she often went up to play at St Thomas's.

'I'm not playing on some old church,' said her cousin Naomi, when she came to stay. 'It's spooky,' Naomi said, before she had even seen it.

'It's not,' Emma said.

'I bet there's ghosts.'

'I've never seen one,' Emma retorted. 'Not up there, at any rate.'

'Where then? Bet you never.'

'Bet what you like. You wouldn't know a ghost if you saw one,' Emma said, and they went off to play in the concrete pipes.

The vicar came to see Dad in July. By September Dad couldn't pretend any longer that his finger was stiff, so all through the autumn he went down to Holy Trinity, two weeks out of three, to play the organ at Matins or Evensong. Mum and Emma, who had never been church-goers, sometimes went along too, to lend him moral support, and often Mr Jarvis visited them to discuss next week's music. Dad found himself playing the organ at choir practices as well, at weddings and funerals, and then suddenly it was November, and the vicar began to talk about Christmas carols.

Winter had come early that year. The vicar stood on the frosty doorstep, staring at the black sky and the burning blue stars, while his breath steamed in the light from the hall, and the hall grew

colder and colder. Mum and Emma huddled round the boiler in the kitchen and wished that Dad were brave enough to boot the vicar out and shut the door. At last they heard the roar of his two-stroke as he shot away down the hill.

'One of these nights he'll come off at that bend by the bridge,' Mum said, hopefully, as Dad came back into the hall and shut the door.

'He thinks there'll be snow before Christmas,' Dad said, rushing to the boiler with his purple hands held out in front of him, like a rocket-powered sleepwalker. 'Says he can smell it.'

'All right for some,' Mum said. 'They've got central heating at the vicarage.'

'He wants to go carol singing,' said Dad.

'I can just see that,' said Mum. 'I can just see him belting round the country on his Yamaha, singing "Silent Night" fit to raise the dead.'

'Not by himself,' Dad said. 'He thinks we should all go out with the three church choirs and tramp round Ockney and Cawley as well. Candle lanterns and mulled ale and Jack Pewsey with his clarinet.'

'Jack plays hot jazz,' Mum pointed out.

'I should think we could cool him down enough for a few carols.'

'The weather'll do that,' Mum said.

'It had better. If it's not Jack Pewsey it'll be me with a portable harmonium and four boy scouts to pull it.'

'The Baptists at Ockney have a harmonium,' said Mum. 'It sounds like a string quartet in a drain.'

'I know—I'll go down to the *Three Compasses* and buy Jack a few pints,' said Dad.

Emma said, 'If you go carol singing, can I come?'

'We'll all come,' Mum said. She turned to Dad who was putting on his parka. 'The vicar wasn't here last Christmas, was he?'

'Came just before Easter. I remember the first time I saw him—lurking under the lych-gate on Good Friday.'

'Then someone ought to tell him about the Waits. He shouldn't upset the Waits.'

The vicar's idea caught on. Everybody in Ockney, Cawley and Strang wanted to go out carol singing at Christmas, although not

67

all of them wanted to go with the vicar. Strang Women's Institute decided to dress up in Old Tyme clothes and go round with a sled, distributing tea and sugar to the Old Age Pensioners. Cawley Comprehensive got up a rival scheme involving Christmas puddings, while the Ockney Baptists wheeled out their portable harmonium and began rehearsing on their own account. On still evenings it could be heard even by the nightwatchman up at Featherstone's Marine Diesels. The vicar became concerned by the threat of so much competition and planned a campaign to eliminate it. He called a meeting in the parish room at Strang, to explain his strategy.

He had brought along a map of the three parishes, divided up into zones with red lines and arrows. Emma, looking at it, was reminded of a plan for battle. She could picture Mr Jarvis lying in ambush with his carol singers armed and hidden behind a hedge, waiting for the Ockney Baptists to come wheezing by. The vicar explained what the red lines were for.

'Carol singing starts a week before Christmas. The W.I. are going round Cawley and Ockney on the twentieth and twenty-third, and Strang on the twenty-second. Cawley Comp will be in Ockney on the twenty-first, Strang on the twenty-third, and at home on the twenty-second. Ockney Baptists will be in Strang on the twenty-first, and Ockney and Cawley on the twenty-second and twenty-third. How's that for dove-tailing?' said the vicar.

'What about us?' Dad asked.

'Aha,' the vicar said, teeth glistening with satisfaction. 'The united church choirs will be at Ockney on the nineteenth, and Cawley on the twenty-first, but we'll be in Strang on the twentieth. That, you see—if you'll just look at this chart—gives us the first crack at Ockney and Strang. No one will have been round before us.'

'And first crack at the collection,' Dad muttered.

'What about the Waits?' Emma asked. She nudged Dad. 'Mum told you to tell him about the Waits.'

Dad looked embarrassed. 'It's not that simple, Em.'

Emma could believe it. The vicar was not the kind of man to listen to things that he did not want to hear, but she was firm. She prodded her father.

'Go on, Dad.'

Dad coughed. 'Er, Mr Jarvis... is this absolutely final?' he asked, pointing to the map.

'And foolproof,' said the vicar. 'Why, is there a fly in the ointment? Trust you to find it.'

'Not exactly. It's just that the Waits always sing in Strang on the twentieth. It's St Thomas's Eve, you see...'

'Waits? Of course I know it's St Thomas's Eve. What Waits?'

'Waits. You know, the old name for carol singers,' Dad said.

'Ah, yes; Middle English, from Old Norman French *waitier* from the Old French *guaitier*... What about them? We've not had any complaints from them?'

'Well, you wouldn't,' Dad mumbled, 'but they might not like it.'

'Who are these Waits? A music society?'

'You could call them that,' Dad agreed.

'If they wanted to book the twentieth, they should have spoken up. I announced the provisional dates ten days ago. No one said anything. Who's their chairman, or secretary, or whatever they have?'

'I don't think they have one,' said Dad. 'They're not an official society, just local people who like to come together to sing carols on St Thomas's Eve. It's a kind of tradition,' he said, lamely.

'They're perfectly welcome to join our band,' the vicar declared, brisk and reasonable. 'I'll say as much on Sunday.'

On Sunday, at Evensong, he announced that the Waits would be very welcome to come carol singing with the united church choirs of Ockney, Cawley and Strang, on the twentieth of December, but not on any other night, and not on their own.

'We don't want clashes between rival supporters,' the vicar said, with a jolly smile. There was an uneasy, almost angry, muttering among the congregation.

'I'll be very surprised,' Mum said, under her breath, 'if anyone from Strang turns out for His Nibs on the twentieth.'

School ended on Tuesday the nineteenth, and that evening Mum and Dad and Emma wrapped up warmly, collected Jack Pewsey, who was Emma's headmaster, and Jack's clarinet, and drove over icy roads to Ockney, where they met the three choirs assembled outside the *King's Head*, and sang 'O Come All Ye Faithful' by way of a warm-up, before moving on to render 'The Holly and the Ivy'—with particular emphasis on the line about the playing of the merry organ, to the Baptists, practising in the chapel with their harmonium.

Next day, on the morning of the twentieth, Jack Pewsey rang up, in a hoarse voice, to say that the cold air had got to his lungs and he wouldn't be able to play his clarinet in Strang that night.

'Lungs, my foot,' said Mum. 'He doesn't want to upset the Waits, that's what.'

'Sensible fellow,' Dad said, and rang the vicar.

'I think we'll have to call it a day, tonight,' he said, but the vicar rang up the Ockney Baptists and that afternoon the pastor drove over in his minibus and unloaded the portable harmonium at Emma's front gate, just as Dad was coming home from Featherstone's.

'But won't you need it yourselves?' Dad asked, with wan hope.

'Not till Thursday, thanks to Generalissimo Jarvis,' the pastor said, leaping back into the minibus. He was an athletic man. He had unloaded the harmonium single-handed. It took the combined efforts of Mum, Dad and Emma to move it into the garage.

'No luck,' Dad said. 'I'll have to go through with it.' He looked with loathing at the minibus, skidding round the bend by the bridge. 'Why do clergymen drive so badly? I knew this mad monk in Macclesfield—he had a Volvo...'

'We'll come too,' Emma said, firmly. If the Waits turned out for a showdown with the vicar, she wanted to be there to see it.

They gathered under a starry sky in frozen silence, by the west door of Holy Trinity. The choir from St Mary's Ockney was there, and the choir of Cawley All Saints, but from Strang there was no one but Mum, Dad, Emma and the vicar.

'I see,' said Mr Jarvis, peering into the darkness. 'I see.'

'I doubt it,' said Emma's dad, bold after a couple of whiskies with Jack Pewsey who had claimed that his tubes needed flushing and coughed hollowly to prove it. 'The Waits sing tonight.'

'And people in Strang prefer to go out with the Waits rather than support their own church choir?'

'No one goes out with the Waits,' Dad said, 'but it's their night, and no one wants to offend them.'

'They had plenty of warning,' the vicar snapped. He turned to the four boy scouts, harnessed like reindeer to the Baptists' harmonium. 'One, two, three–*heave!*'

The choirs moved off, and did not halt until they reached the bridge where Emma's own road went round the corner.

'We'll begin with "Once in Royal David's City",' the vicar announced.

Dad unfolded his camping stool, sat down at the harmonium, and began to play. The choirs began to sing. After they had finished with Royal David's City the scouts went round knocking on doors, while Dad struck up 'Good King Wenceslas'. It was a good carol for a cold night, and the choirs sang vigorously, but at the end of every verse Emma could have sworn that somewhere, not too distant, another choir was singing 'Good King Wenceslas', four bars behind.

'"O Little Town of Bethlehem",' the vicar commanded, when they had finished, and they began again. This time there could be no doubt. Somewhere in the streets of Strang, another choir was singing; *not* 'O Little Town of Bethlehem'. When 'O Little Town of Bethlehem' was over, they all paused to listen. Across the frosty rooftops chimed the strains of a carol that Emma had never heard before, but rather liked:

> '*Out of your sleep arise and wake,*
> *For God mankind now hath y-take,*
> *All of a maid without any make:*
> *Of all women she beareth the bell.*
> *Nowell, nowell, nowell . . .*'

'It seems we have competition,' the vicar remarked, redundantly, when the carol was over. 'Time we moved on, I think.' He chivvied the scouts back into position, and the group slithered over the glistening pavement in the swinging yellow light of the vicar's lantern, which he bore before them on a pole. As they went they heard, apparently from the lane beyond the market, the baying of deep male voices, very loud, very confident.

'My word,' Dad said, blandly, 'the Boar's Head Carol. Haven't heard them singing that for years.'

They stopped at the corner by the service station. '"While Shepherds Watched",' bellowed the vicar, so they sang it, while a single voice, sharp as splitting ice, cut through their chorus:

'Gabriel from heaven-king
Sent to the maiden sweet,
Brought he this blissful tiding,
And fair he gan her greet.'

'Move on!' the vicar shouted. 'This is getting beyond a joke. Move on!'

As they approached the deserted market square a light was seen, bobbing up Brewer's Street, above a cluster of dark figures.

'Could this be our friends, the Waits?' the vicar inquired, nastily, and raising his own lantern on its pole, he strode to meet his rivals, while the choir and the harmonium, conductorless, floundered through 'See, Amid the Winter's Snow'. Emma shuffled her cold feet in their cold boots and stopped singing to hear what would happen. One by one the rest of the choir fell silent as the vicar and the Waits met at last, outside Woolworth's.

'Merry Christmas,' the vicar cried, not at all merry. The Waits stood and faced him, all in a lump. Their lantern shone over their heads, greenish, not glowing.

'I'm sorry it's come to a confrontation,' said the vicar, 'but we gave you plenty of warning. You were cordially invited to join us, and there were notices saying as much put up in the church porch, the Post Office, and outside the police station.'

The leader of the Waits, a huge muffled man in a heavy coat, or cloak, stepped forward a pace, but still no one spoke. The vicar stepped back.

'We'd still be delighted,' he said, less certainly, 'if you'd care to join forces but if not, I really must ask you to move on. It's not as if,' he added, 'you were even singing the same carols as us. Indeed,' he went on, 'I'm not sure that what you are singing *are* carols. I've never heard...'

As one man, the Waits moved; forward, sideways, and disappeared. It looked very much as if they'd gone into Woolworth's, but that could not have been so, because Woolworth's closed at five-thirty, and it was now twenty minutes to nine.

'I think this has gone far enough,' said the vicar, after an awkward silence. 'A joke is a joke, but this is no joke. Who are they?'

'Well, we don't know any of them by name,' Dad said. 'We just call them the Waits. We always have.'

'Since when?'

Mum broke in. 'Since thirteen forty-eight, that's when.'

'The year of the Black Death? This has been going on since *thirteen forty-eight*?'

'I did tell you it was a tradition,' Dad said, self-righteously.

'You didn't tell me what kind of a tradition. Some of those carols are six hundred years old.'

'So are the carol singers,' said Mum.

There was a long pause. The scouts hopped about on frozen toes.

'Nonsense,' said the vicar, at last. 'Carol singing as we understand it was unknown before the fifteenth century. How do you account for that?'

'They're a progressive crowd,' Dad said. 'They've picked up quite a lot of contemporary stuff since they d—since the Black Death. Jack Pewsey says he heard them having a go at "In the Bleak Midwinter" last year—by Holst, you know. They don't really mind what they sing, as long as it's got a good tune. The true essence of carol singing, wouldn't you say?' he asked, with a mild smile.

Far away, from the general direction of Featherstone's Marine Diesels, came a last defiant burst of song.

> *'Welcome be thou, heaven-king,*
> *Welcome, born in one morning,*
> *Welcome for whom we shall sing,*
> *Welcome Yule!'*

There were no more carols that night. There was no more singing at all, but later, in the early hours of the morning, Emma was woken by a fearful row coming from the streets outside. She went into her parents' room and found Mum and Dad in dressing gowns, standing by the window and looking down into the road.

'I could have told him this would happen,' Dad said, as Emma crept alongside.

'Yes, but I notice you didn't,' said Mum.

'No good flogging a dead horse,' Dad said. 'Still, he may pay attention next year. What on earth have they got down there?'

'Nothing on *earth*,' said Mum.

74

'It sounds like iron kettles and ladles.'

'I suppose it would be.'

'Rough music.'

Emma looked out into the street. In the moon's light she could see a steady surge of people passing by, silent themselves but raising a deafening clangour from pots and pans, tongs, hammers and billhooks that they carried.

'I think you'd better have another word with our Mr Jarvis in the morning,' Mum yelled, above the racket.

'D'you think it'll be necessary? After all, they've made their point. They've been carol singing for six centuries, now. They're not going to stop because some hot-rod vicar tries to run Christmas like the Normandy landings.'

'And warn him about Midsummer's Eve.'

'Midsummer Eve's none of his business,' said Dad, 'or mine. Lord alone knows how long *that's* been going on.'

Emma slipped back to her own room and lay listening to the Waits as they came down from Strang St Thomas to play rough music round the vicarage until dawn broke on St Thomas's Day. Through the clashing of iron on iron she heard voices raised, although she could not make out a tune. Whatever they were chanting, however, it was not a Christmas carol.

A Lot of Mince-pies

Robert Swindells

I wish to God I'd never heard of the school choir, and I'm not the only one. In three days' time we'll go carolling round the village, same as every year. We'll work our melodious way along the high-street, trekking up gravel driveways to do our stuff and knock for donations. All proceeds to local charities. We'll do all the posh houses on Micklebarrow Close, then the Red Lion and the supermarket car-park. The supermarket'll be open late and seething with last-minute shoppers as it always is on Christmas Eve. We never fail to make a killing there. And after that we'll move out to where the street-lamps end and do some of the cottages and a farm or two. The cottages are a dead loss as far as money's concerned, but school choirs have sung outside them since just after the dinosaurs and we carry on the tradition. The farms are better. They know we're coming so they keep the dogs in and do hot mince-pies and ginger wine for us. I can't stand mince-pies.

Anyway, from the minute we troop out of the schoolyard behind old Exley at seven o'clock, the kids'll be waiting for one thing. They'll be waiting for the last house—the Meltons' place, with its tangled garden, crumbling brick, and funny little windows. It's three-quarters of a mile from the village, and the choir usually gets there about nine o'clock. The Meltons'll be waiting, and as soon as we strike up the first number they'll open the door and stand there in carpet-slippers, smiling and swaying a little to the music. They're the most ancient couple you're ever likely to see—my mum says they were old when she was in the choir—but the thing about them is, you can actually see that they're enjoying the carols, and afterwards they make a generous donation and give presents to all the kids. There's always eighteen in the choir and I suppose the Meltons buy the stuff on their Christmas shopping expedition, but I don't know where they go—nobody ever sees them in the village. The presents aren't tatty either—none of your quid-a-dozen made in Taiwan plastic rubbish. They tend to be things like cartridge pens, penknives and wallets and purses made of real leather. Last year I got a calculator. As soon as the singing's over they beckon some kid inside— someone whose face they've taken a fancy to I suppose—and the chosen one reappears a few minutes later with a double armful of little packets.

By now you'll be thinking this sounds like the perfect end to Christmas Eve and wondering why I'm moaning. Hang about, and I'll tell you what happened last year.

It was a clear, starry night, and the hoar-frost was already forming on the grass as we left the last of the farms behind and set off to sing for the Meltons. The fields were sheets of silver and the hedges were black and I slackened my pace till a gap opened between me and the others. It was very still and quiet, and suddenly I got this feeling that once, on a frosty night long ago, somebody like me had passed this way alone. I don't know what brought it on but it was a heck of a strong feeling—like being haunted without actually seeing anything. I shivered, and then a wave of sadness hit me for that unknown walker, long since dead. It must have been the quiet that did it—that or the moonlight. Anyway it rattled me, and I was glad when Shaun Wrigley noticed I wasn't with the party and turned, shouting to me to get a move on.

We got to the Meltons' place at ten past nine. One downstairs window strained pale light through its curtain but the garden was black. The gate had no top hinge and old Exley had to lift it before he could open it. It squealed, and when he dropped it there were glove-prints in its coating of frost.

Beyond the gate, some sunflowers had blown over. Their dried-out heads hung low across the path. They nodded and crackled as we waded through them. One snapped off and Shaun Wrigley booted it. It cartwheeled up the path shedding seeds, then veered off into long grass. We formed an arc around the door, shuffling and clearing our throats. Our breath hung in clouds round our heads.

'Right, folks?' old Exley whispered. He only called us folks on Christmas Eve. '"Hark the Herald", after two.' He counted us in and we were away.

They must have been waiting behind the door, because halfway through line three the latch clicked and it swung inwards and there they were, him with his arm round her shoulder, nodding in time with the music. You couldn't tell if they were smiling because what light there was was behind them, but you got the impression that they were.

We went through our repertoire, making a pretty good job of it. My feet got so cold standing still I couldn't feel them, but I didn't mind. It was our last stint, and in ten minutes or so I'd be on my way home with the job behind me for another year and a nice little gift in my pocket.

Our last number was 'We Wish You a Merry Christmas'. Nobody could accuse us of originality. As the final note died away, the Meltons clapped. They always did that. Then the old guy flapped a hand and said, 'Let that one come in—the one with the bobble-cap.' We were all bunched together so you couldn't tell who he meant, and I'd forgotten I had my pom-pom hat on so I didn't move. Old Exley craned over the kids' heads, trying to see where old Melton was pointing. He spotted my pom-pom and said, 'Wake up, lad—the gentleman's waiting.'

I hurried forward, feeling myself go red. As I did so this third-year girl, Stephanie Williams, said something I didn't catch and made a half-hearted grab for my sleeve. She had a funny look on her face but she's a peculiar girl at the best of times and I just sort of jerked my arm out of her reach and brushed past. It wasn't till I was inside with my hat in my hand that I remembered Stephanie'd been the chosen one last year.

I was standing in a stone-flagged passageway. To my left a door stood ajar. Light trickled feebly from beyond it, falling in a wedge across the flags. I saw slug-trails and there was a flat, fungoid smell.

The old woman slipped a hand under my elbow and began steering me along the passageway. Beyond the puddle of light I was virtually blind. Behind me, the old man closed the door.

'This way, my dear.' The woman guided me to the foot of some wooden stairs that went up into blackness. I didn't want to insult them or hurt their feelings or anything, but the creepiness of the place was getting to me and I hung back a bit. 'Is there a light?' I ventured.

'Oh, no, dear.' She sounded surprised—shocked, almost. The

old man, shuffling after us said, 'He can't do with the light, you see.'

'Who?' My scalp prickled. We began climbing the uncarpeted stairs.

'Why Gilbert of course,' said the woman. 'Our little son. He can't do with it, can he, Daddy?'

'No, Mummy,' her husband replied. 'He's a good boy, but he can't do with the light at all.'

As we ascended the air grew colder and the rank smell more intrusive. The woman's fingers felt like claws in the crook of my elbow, and suddenly I wanted to break free and run for it. I didn't, because the man was right behind us and because I didn't fancy looking like a wally in front of the choir. Instead I said, 'I didn't know you had a boy.' My voice sounded shaky, even to me.

'Oh, yes,' crooned the woman. 'We've had him ever such a long time haven't we, Daddy?'

'A long, long time, Mummy,' old Melton confirmed, and it occurred to me that they were probably mad. It was Christmas Eve and here I was in the dark with a pair of decrepit lunatics who thought they had a kid called Gilbert.

At the top of the stairs was a creaky landing. It was not completely dark, because there was a door with about an inch of bluish light showing under it. Mrs Melton let go my arm and whispered, 'Gilbert's room. I'll open the door, and you can pop in and give him his present.'

'Present?' A mixture of dread and embarrassment scrambled my brain. I had no present. Was I supposed to have? Perhaps a gift for Gilbert was part of the yearly ritual. If so, nobody'd told me. I flushed in the chill gloom, stammering, 'I–I'm sorry, Mrs Melton. I didn't know. I haven't–'

'Yes, you have.' I started as the old man, who must have crept up behind me, hissed in my ear. His breath smelled vile.

The only thing I had was my hat, now a damp, screwed-up lump in my hands. I remembered he'd mentioned it outside. The one with the bobble cap. Stupidly, I held it out. 'This–you mean this?' He chuckled.

'A kiss,' he whispered. 'Only a kiss, under the mistletoe.'

'I'm a boy,' I croaked, appalled. 'I don't kiss other boys.'

He didn't reply.

The woman stretched up and drew a bolt near the top of the

door. It grated and slammed. As the echo died I heard something else–an uncouth, wordless cry from the room beyond, and I knew then that Gilbert was real and that there must be something horribly wrong with him. She bent and drew a second bolt.

I don't know why I didn't turn then and run. I'll never know. I only know I've spent every day since wishing I had.

The door swung inward. 'Gilbert,' the woman crooned. 'Here's somebody with a present for you, darling.' I couldn't see past her. The old man laid an arm across my shoulders and pushed me forward. I was half resisting and he really had to exert pressure. He kept murmuring, 'Come along–come along,' as though he was talking to a stubborn infant. If I'd dug my heels in he wouldn't have stood a chance, but even now a part of me was scared of hurting their feelings. A mistletoe kiss seems such a small thing, and how do you tell parents nicely that the thought of being in the same room with their kid makes you want to throw up, let alone kissing him?

The woman moved aside. There was a bed. Above the bed a dim blue lightbulb burned. Somebody had fastened a sprig of mistletoe to its dusty, fraying flex. The light fell on rumpled sheets, and on the boy they called Gilbert.

I gaped. God knows what I'd been expecting–some slavering, semi-human monster I suppose, but Gilbert was beautiful. I know it's a funny word to use about a boy but he was. He lay, propped on one elbow, looking at me through dark, liquid, lemur's eyes. His tip-tilted nose cast a smudge of shadow across a mobile mouth. His hair fell in a dark cascade to his shoulders, concealing the hand that supported his head. His frame was lean, his pale skin smooth as cream.

Old Melton dropped his hand to the small of my back and pushed gently. 'Go on now, boy–one little kiss, that's all.'

I moved towards the bed, but it wasn't the old man's hand that made me. It was partly relief of course–relief that I wasn't about to touch some unspeakable horror with my lips, but mostly it was Gilbert's eyes. I read a bit once out of a book my mum was reading. It was a romance, and somebody was going on about drowning in someone's eyes. It struck me as daft at the time but now, when I try to figure out why I permitted what happened that night to happen, I remember Gilbert's eyes and I think I know what that writer meant.

Anyway, I found myself standing by the bed and I couldn't tear my eyes away from his. He didn't say anything but he made a motion with his head and I knew he wanted me to kneel down. I felt sick and weak and unreal. As I went down on one knee I was back in infant school, doing the crib scene in the Nativity Play. I was the first shepherd, kneeling at the manger with the star above and Mary and Joseph behind, watching. It only lasted a second, and then Gilbert leant forward and his lips parted and I saw why he couldn't talk. His mouth was crammed with spikes.

I won't go on about it. As soon as I saw that mouth I knew what he was, but by then it was too late. He took what he wanted from me and now I'm one of them, like Stephanie Williams and the other chosen. We all make the trip out to the Melton place once a month—each on a separate night of course. We have to go, or we'd die like everybody else.

I expect you're wondering what it's like. Well, you don't feel that much different really, except you've no energy and the light hurts and you see colours as sort of faded. There're a lot more of us about than you think, by the way—so many that you're bound to know at least one. He'll be pasty-faced and a bit flabby, and not too particular about his clothes. He'll be irritable a lot of the time and he won't smile much. You'll probably wonder what he does for fun, or if he even knows what fun is. You might wonder why he bothers to go on living at all, and he'll certainly wonder himself sometimes. I do.

And I suppose the answer is that life's precious, and we tend to cling onto it even if we're not enjoying it. Whether I'll feel that way a thousand years from now remains to be seen. A thousand years is a lot of mince-pies.

Ghost Alarm

Nicholas Fisk

The boy–Leo didn't even know his name–stuck his face close to Leo's and jeered, 'What, you're living in Old Farm? Your dad must be barmy, taking that place! It's haunted! Spooked!' He pulled a horrible face and waved his arms, imitating a ghost.

'Spooked!' said another boy, crossing his eyes and sticking out his tongue. 'Always has been! For centuries!' This boy's name was Russ, Leo knew. So far, Leo could name only about half the children in his new school. This did not worry him. At the age of eleven, he had been to half a dozen schools. His father's job took him all over the place: when he moved, the family upped sticks and followed.

A girl called Sharon joined in. 'The family that had Old Farm before you,' she said, 'I knew them. They didn't last long. They *saw things*...!' She shuddered exaggeratedly and rolled her eyes.

'I don't believe in ghosts,' Leo said, flatly. 'Ghosts are for kids.' He pushed through, got his bike from the racks and pedalled steadily through the crowd in the playground. He headed for home. Old Farm. As he rode, he thought, 'You liar! You do believe in ghosts. You're scared stiff of them. Because of the burglar alarm.'

The burglar alarm...

His father, Mike Winters, had installed it himself. He was an electronics engineer. Alarm systems were child's play to him. So he got busy putting pressure pads under carpets–mounting little projectors that put out invisible beams–building, for the living room, a thing like a loudspeaker cabinet that screamed, deafeningly, if you crossed its path. He enjoyed the job. So did Leo, who helped him.

And so did little Emma, Leo's sister. She trotted about offering the wrong tools at the wrong time. '*Scoo*-drive,' she said, when you needed pliers. '*Why*-ah!' she announced, when you particularly

83

didn't want wire. Each time, her father gravely said, 'Why, thank you, Emma!' and took whatever it was she offered. She was only three.

Then the alarm system was all done and it all worked. The tests had been faultless. 'Walk through it, Kathy,' Mike told his wife. She walked, bells rang. 'Come towards me, Emma!' Emma earnestly walked and the loudspeaker cabinet alarm bellowed its head off. Leo and Mike smiled smugly.

Kathy said, 'Look, Mike, we'll all die of heart failure if those things are going to go off every time we make a move.'

'But Kathy, don't you see!—you never *will* hear them. Not unless we get intruders. That's the whole idea.' He made a sidelong face at Leo—a face that meant, '*Women...*' Leo said, 'Honestly, Mum. Never a sound.'

He and his father couldn't have been more mistaken.

That very night, in the pitch darkness, bells rang and the siren yelled.

Shocked out of sleep, everyone leapt out of bed. Mike said 'Stay back!' and ran down the staircase. He gripped an ebony club in his hand, a wicked weapon he had picked up in Africa. Leo shone his powerful spotlamp out of an upstairs window. The spot scanned empty fields. Kathy clutched Emma to her. The house seemed to shake with the noise of the alarms.

They found nothing and nobody. No burglars, no ghosts, no intruders. And, in the morning, not a trace of them outside: no damaged window frames, no footsteps in the soft earth.

Mike left early for the airport and a plane to France. Leo went to school. Kathy and Emma were alone in the house...

The alarms went off. First, at eleven in the morning. 'Impossible,' Kathy said. 'They're set to work only at night.' She switched off the din.

They went off again in the afternoon. Twice. The second time, Kathy burst into tears, driven to distraction by the awful, head-bursting noise. Emma consoled her and she soon recovered.

Leo came back from school and checked everything. All was in order, yet the alarms had gone off. How was that possible? He thought of ghosts, and shivered.

That night, the alarms went off four times. Leo pushed the cancel button and, holding his father's ebony club, gritted his teeth and looked for intruders. After the third false alarm, Kathy brandished a pair of scissors and shouted, 'Enough! I'm going to cut the wires!' 'For heaven's sake don't!' Leo cried. 'The system's tamper-proof! Cut the wires and it will go on for ever!' Kathy, white-faced and shaken, went to bed.

Leo, making a final check, heard a small noise–turned–and saw Emma, standing behind him in her nightie. 'Burglar,' she said. 'Over there!' She pointed her finger at the place where the loudspeaker alarm stood.

Leo's spine iced. The lights were on in the living room yet he could see nothing. 'Where? Where?' he shouted.

'Gone now,' Emma said, calmly.

'Why, you little . . . !' Leo began. He almost wanted to brain her with the club. 'If you think that's funny!'

'He was over there,' Emma said, wide-eyed and serious. She pointed to the same place.

Leo swallowed his anger and made tea. Emma silently got the mugs. She said, 'I did see the burglar. I really did.'

'You didn't. You're just a little show-off liar.'

She wasn't listening. 'I thought burglars was robber men,' she said. 'I thought they was people, like us.'

'They are. Here, take this up to Mum and don't spill it.'

At the door, she turned and said, 'Our burglar isn't a robber man. He's not proper. He's like glass. And no clothes on. Just glass, and milky.' She was on her dignity.

Leo thought of ghosts. And again shivered.

During the next day, the alarm went off twice in the day. Kathy rang a neighbour and asked about local hotels.

In the night it went off three times. The family gave up all hope of sleep. They dozed in the living room. Emma kept looking at the place where the loudspeaker alarm stood.

When the third false alarm sounded, Kathy said, 'I can't stand it! I just can't! We're leaving, I'll call a taxi . . .'

Emma said, 'We can't leave the poor burglar. He's lost. He told me so. He wants to go home . . .'

'Don't, Emma. I'm not in the mood for fairy stories. Just do as you're told.'

'He's only little, he's not much bigger than me. I've seen him three times, four times. Over there. He's lost . . .'

Kathy grabbed Emma's shoulders and started shaking her. Then the alarm went off yet again and Kathy began screaming, holding Emma to her. Emma only half noticed what her mother was doing. Her eyes were fixed on something, or nothing, a little way away.

'It's all right,' she murmured to this thing. 'I've got an idea. *Father Christmas.*'

Leo packed his own suitcase, then helped Kathy pack hers. Her hands were trembling, even her face trembled. 'We're leaving,' she kept saying. 'Getting out. Leaving.'

In the living room, Emma talked wordlessly with the 'burglar'. Following its instructions, she carefully freed the wires leading to the loudspeaker alarm from the skirting boards. This done, she carried the speaker to the fireplace with its wires attached. It was heavy work for her. Her face was pink.

She placed the cabinet in the fireplace, face up. Getting it positioned just right took her some time but she persevered. When she finished, she nodded and said, 'Father Christmas!' She waited for an answer–apparently got it–and said, 'Yes, that's right. He'll come.'

Father Christmas, she knew, was what the burglar needed. Father Christmas was waiting, just as he waited for her list of Christmas presents, above the chimney. You wrote your list with Mum's help; set fire to it; and Father Christmas somehow read the sparks. Then you got your presents.

It worked for Emma: it would work for the burglar. The burglar wanted to send a message to somewhere up in the sky. Now he could. Father Christmas would hear him.

'All done,' she told the burglar. She knew he understood for he reached out to her–stretched out his glassy, milky limbs. He was sort of under-watery, Emma thought, moving so slowly and feebly. More like a ghost than a burglar. She put out her plump little hand as if to stroke the thing. It was very close to her now, much closer than ever before...

The burglar alarm sounded. The noise was awful, Emma had to shield her ears with her hands. The alarm in the fireplace was the worst...

And then her mother was rushing down the stairs screaming, 'Out! Get out! I can't stand any more! We'll meet the taxi along the road, get out!' Emma found herself being pulled along like one of the suitcases, dragged along by her mother in the damp night, down the road.

In the house the alarms jangled and screeched and howled. The loudspeaker alarm in the fireplace sent one particular frequency of its noise straight up into the sky—a scream that arrowed through Earth's atmosphere, speared into outer space.

The spaceship picked up the signal. 'Ah!' said its commander—a fragile, glassy, milky being with many limbs—'Ah! We've found him at last!'

In the road near Old Farm, the taxi arrived. Over Old Farm, the spaceship descended. It was glassy, milky, ghostly. It hovered long enough to pick up the crew-member lost for two Earth centuries. It rose, slowly at first but then so fast that clouds were torn to rags.

Only Emma saw it come and go. Only she had been expecting it, or something like it. She looked out of the back window of the taxi, saw the clouds tear and swirl, then heal themselves. She waved and bounced up and down on the seat.

'The burglar's gone,' she said. 'He's gone away so we can go back.' The others ignored her. She tried another tack. 'Suppose Dad telephones,' she said loudly, 'and nobody answers because we're all gone!'

Her mother gasped. 'Oh, I hadn't thought of that! He'd think—I don't know what he'd think! Driver, turn round, take us back!'

These days, no one talks of the Old Farm ghost. The white-painted windows twinkle, the roses Kathy planted flourish. The old house is bright, welcoming, unghostly. Mike refuses to leave. He likes his home.

The burglar alarm is still in circuit. Mike brushes the dust off it now and then and tests it. It always works perfectly.

Leo is becoming seriously interested in electronics. Ghosts aren't his thing.

And Emma? Nobody really believed her talk of spaceships and ghosts. Not even her. She is five now. Next month she is going to her first school. It is all she thinks about.

Christmas in the Rectory

Catherine Storr

It was my great-aunt who told me this story. She had known the people concerned, though I think she had never visited the rectory itself. It is a very old story. It took place more than a hundred years ago.

My great-aunt's especial friend was Kate, who, when she was a nearly grown-up young lady, had gone with her sister Elspeth to stay with their brother and his family in Cornwall for Christmas. William was a parson; a month or so earlier, he had taken charge of a small parish near the sea. Kate and Elspeth had never been to Cornwall, but they had heard that it was a wild sort of country, with a great bare moor in the middle, and all around high cliffs and jagged rocks and roaring seas. So they were surprised to find their brother's rectory a solid grey granite box of a house, more suitable to a city terrace than to remote country, standing alone in a small valley, well planted with trees and shrubs. They could see, from the bent and twisted trees, how strong the blustering winds could be on that coast; but on the day they arrived, though it was the middle of December, the air was still and vaporous under a leaden sky.

This much, and the glossy leaves of the massive rhododendron bushes surrounding the house like a green tide which threatened to engulf the lower windows, was all that the sisters could make out in the fading light of a winter afternoon, as William drove them up to the front door. While he took the pony and chaise round to the stables, his wife, Fanny, welcomed the girls and proposed to show them the room they were to occupy, and then the rest of the house. The two small children at first followed their mother silently, staring at their young aunts with solemn eyes; but soon they remembered that Kate and Elspeth had been welcome playmates not so very long ago, and they began to chatter and to take their part in the guided tour of the house, showing their own

particular possessions. 'That's my chair, and that's Emmy's.' 'This is my best dolly.' 'Here's my horse, his tail is made of real hair.' 'That's my bed, that's nurse's.' This was Emmy in the night-nursery.

'Hugh is such a big boy now, he sleeps in the other nursery by himself,' Fanny said, and Kate thought there was a note of reassurance in her voice as if Hugh perhaps needed consolation for having had to leave the comfort of sharing a night-nursery with nurse and Emmy. But he seemed pleased to show them his new bed, looking very small in a corner of the large day nursery, which, in spite of the fire flickering in the grate and the closely pulled curtains, felt chilly. Yes, Fanny agreed in answer to Elspeth's inquiry, it was a difficult house to keep warm. Even now, when the weather was so unseasonably mild, there were cold draughts in the rooms and passages, and an all-pervading odour of damp. William was sure it was nothing but the sea air that she was smelling, and perhaps he was right. It was true, before their arrival, the house had been standing empty for some months.

'And you've been here such a short time! When you've lived here for longer it will dry out and feel different,' Elspeth said.

'I hope so,' was Fanny's only reply, and it seemed to Kate that it was spoken without conviction. But they had come now to the head of the stairs, and Fanny, going ahead with Emmy, was saying, 'Now we'll show you the little sitting room where we're all going to have tea.'

Hugh put a hand confidingly in Kate's and they followed Fanny downstairs. On the half-landing Kate noticed a door which Fanny hadn't opened for them on their way up and asked, 'Where does that lead to?'

Hugh didn't answer. Instead he pulled her towards the lower flight, as if in a hurry to gain the hall. Kate allowed herself to be led, but asked again, 'What's behind that door?'

Fanny turned to answer over her shoulder. 'It isn't a proper room. It's a sort of half-finished attic over William's study. I keep the door locked because...' She broke off to say gently to Hugh, who was preparing for a tremendous spring down the last four steps, 'Gently, Hugh. You mustn't interrupt Mamma.' Then she went on. 'It's very dark. There aren't any windows, and the roof comes down so low you can't stand upright. There's a trap-door

91

in the floor, too, and I don't want one of the children getting it open and falling through.'

Hugh's leap having been accomplished and duly admired, Fanny opened the door into a small room where tea things were laid in front of a comfortable-looking fire. 'Come in and get warm. The children are going to have tea with us for a treat.'

Certainly Hugh and Emmy did justice to the toast and tea and seedcake. But Kate, remembering that convulsive clutch of her hand on the stairs, observed Hugh and thought that he was still uneasy. He seemed to her to be looking frequently towards the room door, and sure enough, before the children's nurse had appeared there to carry them off to bed, he had disappeared, and did not show himself when called.

Fanny found him, crouching between the end of the sofa and the wall.

'Bedtime, Hugh. Go upstairs with Agnes,' she said.

'No. Won't! Don't want to!'

'Hugh! You know what Papa said?'

Whatever William had said, it was enough to bring Hugh out of hiding, and to make him follow Agnes very slowly towards the door, the corners of his mouth drooping.

'You come up to see me in bed, Mamma?'

'Yes. I'll come and say good night to you when you're safe in bed.'

'I don't remember Hugh being difficult about going to bed last year,' Kate said when the children had left the room.

'He isn't used to the house yet,' Fanny said. She began to put the tea things together.

'Won't one of the maids do that?' Elspeth asked.

'The maids don't stay here at night. They are all village girls and they go home to sleep,' Fanny said.

'Nurse too?'

'No, Agnes doesn't come from the neighbourhood. She came down here with us. The children are very fond of her. We shall miss her dreadfully when she goes.'

'Why is she leaving?' Kate asked.

Fanny corrected herself. 'I should have said *if* she goes. She hasn't really settled here yet and she talks of finding another place. But I hope I shall be able to persuade her to stay.' Fanny carried the tray out of the room and put an end to the conversation.

'Do you think Fanny's happy here?' Kate asked her sister, as they were changing their dress before supper.

'Why shouldn't she be?'

'I'm not sure. There's something... It's not just the house being damp or not having any servants in the evenings. She keeps on looking at the children...'

'You're imagining things. Like that time we went to see all those big stones on top of a hill somewhere. You said you felt they were evil. Remember?' Elspeth said. She opened the door of their bedroom and went out, calling back, 'Hurry up! You'll be late for supper. We're having it in William's study, remember.'

Supper, eaten by a good fire in the long, low study, might have reassured Kate, if she had seen that Fanny was relaxed as she surely had been when the sisters had stayed with the family before. There were occasions when Fanny appeared not to have heard remarks addressed to her. She was preoccupied, almost as if she were listening for some expected sound outside the room. Half-way through the meal, she abruptly got up and left the room; they heard her hasty steps on the stairs and, through the open door, the sound of a child crying. William made a sound of annoyance.

'Hugh again!' he said.

'What's the matter? Can't he sleep?' Kate asked.

'He has got into a bad habit of crying out after he has been put to bed. I have told Fanny that he must not be indulged. He must learn to control himself,' William said.

'But if he's really frightened?' Kate said.

'There is nothing for him to be frightened of. I have asked him what makes him cry out and he cannot explain. Fanny allows him to leave his bedroom door open and she leaves a candle burning in the passage, though I have told her I think this is giving in to weakness. He should fight his fear. If he is afraid,' William said.

When Fanny reappeared she reported that she had left Hugh calmer. It had been another of his bad dreams, he had woken up screaming and terrified. Now Agnes was sitting with him till he should go to sleep.

'He shouldn't be allowed to form the habit of having someone stay with him all the evening,' William said.

'He can't be left alone in that state,' Fanny said.

'He calls out to you to draw attention to himself,' William said.

'No, William, it's not that. You've seen him when he wakes up like this. He's wild with terror. He has real, horrible nightmares.'

'What does he dream about?' Elspeth asked. Neither William nor Fanny answered. Kate saw them glance at each other and she knew that some unspoken message, which she and Elspeth did not understand, was passing between husband and wife.

Both sisters slept soundly that night, a heavy, dreamless sleep from which they woke with difficulty. But in the daylight of the next morning, Kate began to think that she must have been over-tired and fanciful the night before. Fanny seemed less anxious, and Hugh was triumphant and apparently carefree, leading his aunts down to visit 'his' beach, to watch him trying to make a great crab emerge from under its protective overhang of rock, and showing how well he could negotiate the long tongues of black spiked rocks which ran out into the ocean. The only disappointment was that there was still no wind. The sea lay smooth and white under the low, overcast sky, and the shore was silent, except for the whisper and the suck of the water where it met the sand, like the murmur of a conspiracy, a secret, not to be overheard.

In the afternoon, William walked the sisters to the village, a huddle of cottages and an inn near the squat grey tower of the church. There wasn't much to admire inside the building. Kate and Elspeth walked round, looking at the old-fashioned high box pews, reading the memorial tablets on the walls and sympathizing with William's regrets that there was not enough money to put the place into good order. Leaving their brother to discuss the music for the Christmas services with the church harmonium player, they wandered out into the churchyard, where a fine thin rain was shrouding the trees and hedges in a white veil. An elderly man, sweeping up dead leaves from between the neglected graves, stopped his work and stared curiously at them as they approached.

'Good day!' Elspeth called as they approached him.

He eyed them curiously. 'You be Parson's sisters?'

'Yes, we are. We've come to spend Christmas with him,' Elspeth said.

'Haven't been here before, have you?'

'No, this is our first time...'

'That's what I reckoned,' the man said.

'But we'll be coming back again. In the summer, when the weather's better.'

The man shook his head. 'Parson won't stay that long,' he said.

'Of course he will! He's only been here two months.'

'He won't, though. They don't stay,' the man said.

'Who don't stay?'

The man leant his broom against a mausoleum with a large urn on its massive lid. 'Did you see that tablet in church? List of all the parsons that's ever been here?'

'I saw it, but I didn't read all the names,' Elspeth said.

'If you had, you'd ha'seen. Not a one of them stopped out the year. Not since *he* was here, and that's more'n seventy years gone.'

'Who was *he*?'

'I'm not speaking his name. You won't find it up on that tablet, either. A real bad one he was, according to what they say. But for all that, he was parson here. Twenty-five years he was here. Terrible years they was, too.'

'What did he do? What happened to him?' Elspeth asked, fearfully.

'Hanged hisself, didn't he? In his own house. Over the room he was building where Parson has his study,' the man said, with a ghoulish pleasure in shocking.

'*Hanged* himself?'

'Or his Master did it for him, more like. My father used to say he'd sold hisself to...' He stopped abruptly as William's voice came across the churchyard. 'Elspeth! Kate! We should be getting back before the dark.'

'What did your father say he'd done?' Elspeth asked quickly, but the man had turned away. Over his shoulder, he said 'Nothing. And don't you go telling Parson I said anything. It's only a pack of silly stories. Some folk'd believe anything.' He picked up his broom and shuffled off as William appeared at the end of the path.

'You're cold! I shouldn't have let you stay out in this damp spot for so long,' he said. As they turned in the direction of the Rectory, he said, 'I saw you talking to old Johnstone. What was he telling you?'

'We were telling him we'd love to see this place in the summer. If you're still here,' Elspeth said before Kate could answer.

'Why shouldn't I still be here?' William asked.

'He seemed to think you wouldn't be staying for long. He didn't explain why.'

'I see no reason why he should think that. I have no intention of leaving.'

They walked on in silence. Kate was aware that William was displeased, but she could think of nothing to say to improve the situation. Presently William said, 'Perhaps one of the village girls who work in the house has heard Fanny talking about the children's health, and spread the story that I may not be staying here.'

'Are the children not well?' Kate asked.

'They are perfectly well. Fanny is apt to be nervous about them. I am hoping that she will see there is nothing in this place to give her any anxiety when...' Kate had thought he was going to say, '...when the better weather comes.' But instead, he said, '...when the nights are shorter.' A curious way of putting it, she thought.

She remembered this conversation later in the day, when she again noticed Hugh's behaviour as bedtime approached. For more than an hour before Nurse was due to fetch him and Emmy upstairs, he was uneasy, alternating between long silences and frantic gaiety. When Agnes announced that his bath was ready, Kate offered to go upstairs with him, and half an hour later she was sitting on the side of his bed, looking at his trembling lip and sure that William was wrong. This was a very frightened child.

Fanny came in from the night-nursery and bent to kiss Hugh good night.

'Sleep well, my darling. And Hugh! Don't call out tonight. You know it annoys Papa.'

'But Mamma...'

'I'll come and look at you before I go to bed to make sure you are all right.'

Hugh lay still. But, as Kate and Fanny moved towards the door, he cried out desperately, 'Don't shut the door, Mamma! Don't shut the door!'

'I'm not going to, my dear. Look! I'll leave it like this, so you can see the light from the passage.'

That evening Hugh did not call out for his mamma. But, in the middle of the night, Kate was woken by the screams of a younger child. She opened her room door and saw Fanny coming from the night-nursery, with Emmy in her arms. 'A nightmare. I'm taking her back to my room,' Fanny said, trying to reassure. But, back in bed beside Elspeth who had hardly stirred, Kate lay awake, with that small face contorted with terror before her mind's eye; while in the quiet room the shadows from the dying fire reached out like fingers, advancing and retreating, advancing and retreating, never quite reaching where she lay.

'Do both the children have nightmares?' she asked Fanny the next day.

'They don't sleep as well here as they did in Coombe. They may be better when the weather improves and they can go out and get more fresh air,' Fanny said.

'But Fanny, these dreams...'

Fanny stopped her. 'Dear Kate, don't ask me any more. William is sure I am anxious about nothing. He thinks it is my nervousness which infects the children and induces them to sleep badly. I expect he is right. I ought to have more faith, and to believe that if he has been called to this place, nothing can really go wrong with any of us.'

Kate was still puzzled. But this was the day before Christmas, and there was too much for everyone to do to leave time for fancy or speculation. The children were excited, naughty, charming, in all the places where they were supposed not to be, and never there when they were wanted. They were sufficiently exalted by the mystery of Christmas to go to bed with a fairly good grace; they hung their stockings on the nursery mantelpiece, listened to the Christmas story from their father, and were safely tucked up by seven o'clock. Supper was undisturbed by either child's dreams and, soon after ten o'clock, William and Fanny were persuaded by the two sisters to leave the rest of the preparations to them.

'There's not so much to do. The holly garlands, and I must finish the red frock for Emmy's doll,' Kate said.

'Very well, if you are sure you don't mind. But don't stay up too late! Remember we are all going to have a long, tiring day tomorrow,' Fanny said, as she gratefully took her bedroom candle and left the study. William, five minutes later, repeated the injunction. 'Don't stay up late.'

It was very quiet in the study after Fanny and William had gone. No child cried out tonight. The only sounds were the crackling of the glowing fire, the soft tap of the rhododendron leaves against the windows, and the regular tick of the big grandfather clock in the hall outside. The sisters hardly spoke, both intent on their work. The clock struck eleven, and still they hadn't finished. It was nearly an hour later when Kate put the finishing stitches to the doll's frock, and was just about to ask Elspeth how her work was getting on, when she heard the footsteps.

They were outside the room. At first she thought they were coming down the stairs. Then she realized that they were overhead, in the attic space above the study. She looked across at Elspeth, who had laid down the garland of holly on which she'd been pricking her fingers for the last hour and a half.

'Who?' Kate breathed. But as she spoke, she heard the whine of rusty hinges and from where she sat near the fire, she could see the trap-door in the ceiling of the room slowly lifted.

'It's William! He's come to scold us for being so long down here,' Elspeth said, and without moving, she called out, 'Yes, William, we're just going up. We'll be very quiet, we won't disturb you.'

There was a long silence. No rebuke for their tardiness. No friendly good night. Instead a long blast of cold air swept down from the trap-door. Then the hinges creaked again and the trap was dropped. They heard slow, heavy footsteps pass over their heads. Then silence again.

'Let's go to bed. Quickly,' Elspeth said, and Kate noticed, as they climbed the stairs, their candles shedding small pools of light before them, that Elspeth more than once looked back over her shoulder. Almost as if she was afraid of the dark, which lay like a great ocean behind them. At the last step, a croak and a rattle down below made her cry out, 'What's that?'

'It's the clock clearing its throat before it strikes. There! Midnight! Come *on*,' said Kate.

'You're cold,' said Elspeth, as they lay side by side in the large bed.

'It was chilly down there in the study,' Kate said. But, as she felt her sister's hand, she knew that it hadn't been the perpetual damp of the great grey house which had chilled them both that night.

They woke to shouts from the nursery, the scampering of small bare feet along the corridor, and the morning was taken up with church-going, present-giving, the preparation, and later the eating, of the Christmas feast. The holly garlands were admired, the doll's frock a perfect fit, William and Fanny were delighted with the gifts the sisters had brought from the rest of the family,

Kate and Elspeth were touched and pleased with the presents Fanny had devised for the children to give them. In the general bustle and excitement of the day, they forgot the events of the night before until late in the evening, when, the children safely in bed, tired out with pleasure and feasting, William rose from his easy chair, deciding that he, at least, must go early to bed.

'And you mustn't be late either. You both stayed up late enough last night, working for today,' Fanny said to the two girls.

'We weren't so very late. We went upstairs directly after William called down to us,' Elspeth said.

'I called down to you? What do you mean?' William asked.

'You opened the trap-door up there and told us to go to bed.'

'I certainly did not...'

'No, it wasn't you that called out. It was Elspeth. She called out to you that we were just coming,' Kate said.

'It was just before twelve o'clock. The grandfather in the hall struck as we went up the stairs,' Elspeth said.

'William was asleep before eleven last night,' Fanny said.

'It must have been some other sound you heard. That trap hasn't been opened since we came to the house,' William said.

'We heard your footsteps over the study. Walking along the floor up there. Then the trap-door opened and we thought it must be you, William...'

Fanny was very pale. She said, 'William!', imploring him. Kate said, 'Then there really is something...?' but she didn't finish the sentence. Suddenly she began to understand. The children's fear of the dark. Fanny's nervousness. The refusal of the village girls to spend the night in the house. The half-told tale of the sexton the day before. The cold damp that hung around the rooms in spite of the generous fires. And, as the explanation crept into her mind and illuminated everything she had found mysterious before, she heard William's voice, cracking in its intensity as he asked, 'Kate! Elspeth! When the trap opened... you didn't look up, did you? For God's sake, tell me you didn't look up?'

A Christmas Pudding Improved with Keeping

❦ ⚬ ❦

Philippa Pearce

It was boiling hot weather. The tall old house simmered and seethed in a late heat-wave. The Napper family shared the use of the garden, but today it was shadier and cooler for them to stay indoors, in their basement flat. There they lay about, breathless.

'I wish,' said Eddy, 'I wish—'

'Go on,' said his father. 'Wish for a private swimming-pool, or a private ice-cream fountain, or a private—' He gave up, too hot.

'I wish—' said Eddy, and stopped again.

'Go to the park, Eddy,' said his mother. 'Ask if the dog upstairs would like a walk, and take him to the park. See friends there. Try the swings for a bit of air.'

'No,' said Eddy. 'I wish I could make a Christmas pudding.'

His parents stared at him, too stupefied by heat to be properly amazed. He said: 'I know you always buy our Christmas pudding, Mum, but we could make one. It wouldn't be too early to make one now. We could. I wish we could.'

'Now?' said his mother faintly. 'In all this heat? And why? The bought puddings have always been all right, haven't they?'

'I remember,' said Mr Napper, 'my granny always made her own Christmas puddings. Always.'

'Your granny!' said Mrs Napper.

'She made a batch. I remember them boiling away in her kitchen for hours and hours and hours. She made them almost as early as this—anyway, well before Christmas—and stored them away. When Christmas came, she served a pudding that she'd made and kept from the year before. We always ate pudding that was at least a year old. A Christmas pudding improves with keeping.' He smacked his lips. 'My! Those Christmas puddings!'

Mrs Napper had closed her eyes, apparently in sleep.

101

Eddy said: 'I do wish I could make a Christmas pudding...'

'We children all had a turn at stirring the pudding,' said Mr Napper. 'You wished as you stirred, but you mustn't say what your wish was. And the wish would come true before the next Christmas.'

'Yes!' cried Eddy. 'That's it! I want to stir, and to wish—to wish—'

'Well,' said his mother, with her eyes shut, 'if we ever make our own Christmas pudding, it won't be during a heat-wave.'

'I just wish—' Eddy began again.

'Stop it, Eddy!' said his mother, waking up to be sharp. 'Go to the park. Here's money for ice-cream.'

When Eddy had gone, his father said: 'That settled him!'

His mother said: 'The ideas they get! Come and gone in a minute, though...' They both dozed off.

But the idea that had come to Eddy did not go. Not at all.

The Nappers had moved into their basement flat in the spring of that year. Long, long ago the whole house had been one home, for one family, with servants, or a servant, in the basement kitchen. Then the house had been split up into flats, one floor to a flat, for separate families. Nowadays a whole family lived on the first floor, where the bedrooms had been. Another family lived on the ground floor, where the parlour and dining room had been; and this family shared with the Nappers the use of the back-garden. (As this ground floor family had a baby and a poodle-dog, they made good use of the garden, too.) And the Napper family lived in the basement.

The conversion of the house into flats had been done many years before; but this was the first time since then—although the Nappers were not to know it—that a child had lived in the basement. Eddy was that child.

From their very first moving into the basement, Eddy had had strange dreams. One dream, rather; and not a dream that his dreaming eyes saw, but something that he dreamt he heard. The sound was so slight, so indistinct, that at first even his dreaming self did not really notice it. *Swish-wish-wish!* it went. *Swish-wish-wish*... The dream-sound, even when he came to hear it properly, never woke him up in fright; indeed, it did not frighten him at all. To begin with, he did not even remember it when he woke up.

But—*Swish-wish-wish!*—the sound became more distinct as time passed: more insistent. Never loud, never threatening, however; but coaxing, cajoling, begging—begging and imploring—

'Please,' said Eddy to his mother, 'oh, *please*! It's not a heat-wave now; it's nearly Christmas. And it's Saturday tomorrow; we've got all day. Can't we make our own Christmas pudding tomorrow? Please, please!'

'Oh, Eddy! I'm so busy!'

'You mean we can't?' Eddy looked as if he might cry. 'But we must! Oh, Mum, we must!'

'No, Eddy! And when I say No, I mean, No!'

That evening, as they sat round the gas-fire in their sitting room, there was an alarming happening: a sudden rattle and clatter that seemed to come from above and come down and ended in a crash—a crash not huge but evidently disastrous; and it was unmistakeably in their own basement flat, in their own sitting room.

And yet it wasn't.

Mrs Napper had sprung to her feet with a cry: 'Someone trying to break in!' Her eyes stared at the blank, wall-papered wall from which the crashing sound had seemed to come. There was nothing whatsoever to be seen; and now there was dead silence—except for the frantic barking of the poodle upstairs. (The ground-floor family—mother, father, and baby—had gone out for the evening, leaving the dog on guard; and he hadn't liked what he had just heard, any more than the Nappers had done.)

Eddy rushed to the wall and put his hands flat upon it. 'I wish—' he cried. 'I wish—'

His father pulled him away. 'If there's anybody—or anything—there,' he said, 'I'll get at him.' He knocked furiously on the wall several times. Then he calmed himself and began rapping and tapping systematically, listening intently for any sound of hollowness, and swearing under his breath at the intrusive barking of the dog upstairs.

'Ah!' he said. 'Here we are!' He began scrabbling at the wallpaper with his pocket-knife and his fingernails. Layer upon layer of wallpaper began to be torn away.

'Whatever will the landlord say?' asked Mrs Napper, who had recovered her courage and some of her calm.

Mr Napper said: 'Eddy, get my tool-box. I don't know what may be under here.' While Eddy was gone, Mrs Napper also went to fetch dust-sheets and spread them out against the mess.

What was underneath all the layers of ancient wallpaper was a small, squarish wooden door let into the wall at about waist-level: its knob had gone, but Mr Napper prised it open without too much difficulty. The dog upstairs was still barking; and, as soon as the little door was open, the sound came to them with sudden clearness.

Mr Napper was feeling with one hand through the doorway into the blackness inside. 'There's a shaft in here,' he said. 'It's not wide at all, or deep from front to back; but it seems to go right up. I need the torch, Eddy.'

Even as Eddy came back with the torch, Mr Napper was saying cheerfully: 'We've been making a fuss about nothing. This is just an old-fashioned service-lift, from the time our sitting room was part of a kitchen.'

'A lift?' Eddy repeated.

'Only a miniature one, for hauling food straight up from the kitchen to the dining room, and bringing the dirty dishes down again. It was worked by hand.'

Mrs Napper had not spoken. Now she said: 'What about all that rattling, and the crash?'

Mr Napper was shining his torch into the shaft of the service-lift. 'The ropes for hauling up and down were rotten with age. They gave way at last. Yes, I can see the worn-out ends of the cords.'

'But why should they choose to rot and break now?' asked Mrs Napper. 'Why now?'

'Why not now?' asked Mr Napper; closing that part of the discussion. He was still peering into the shaft. 'There was something on the service-shelf when it fell. There are some bits of broken china; and—this—'

He brought out from the darkness of the square hole an odd-looking, dried-looking, black-looking object that sat on the palm of his hand like an irregularly shaped large ball.

'Ugh!' said Mrs Napper instantly.

Mr Napper said: 'It's just the remains of a ball of something—a composite ball of something.' He picked at it with a finger-nail. 'Tiny bits all stuck and dried together...' He had worried out a fragment, and now he crumbled it in his hand. 'Look!'

Mrs Napper peered reluctantly over his shoulder. 'Well, I must say...'

'What is it?' asked Eddy; but suddenly he knew.

His mother had touched the crumblings with her finger, and then immediately wiped her finger on a corner of dust-sheet. 'It looks like old, old sultanas and raisins and things...'

'That's what I think,' said Mr Napper. 'It's a plum pudding. It *was* a plum pudding.'

Eddy had known: a Christmas pudding.

'But what was it doing there, in that service-lift thing?' asked Mrs Napper. 'Did someone leave it there deliberately; or was it just mislaid? Was any of it eaten, do you think?'

'Hard to tell,' said Mr Napper.

'And why did the workmen leave it there, when they sealed up the shaft, to make the separate flats?' But she was thinking. 'Perhaps it was between floors and they didn't see it.'

'Or perhaps they didn't like to touch it,' said Eddy.

'Why do you say that?' his mother asked sharply.

'I don't know,' said Eddy.

They cleared up the mess as well as they could. The ancient pudding was wrapped in newspaper and put in the waste-bin under the kitchen-sink.

Then it was time for Eddy to go to bed.

That night Eddy dreamt his dream more clearly than ever before. *Swish-wish-wish!* went whatever it was, round and round: *Swish-wish-wish!* In his dream, he was dreaming the sound; and in his dream he opened his eyes and looked across a big old shadowy basement kitchen, past a towering dresser, hung with jugs and stacked with plates and dishes on display–past a little wooden door to a service-lift–past a kitchen range with saucepans and a kettle on it–

His gaze reached the big kitchen table. Someone was standing at the table, with his back to Eddy: a boy, just of Eddy's age and height, as far as he could tell. In fact, Eddy had the strangest, dream-sensation that he, Eddy, was standing there at the kitchen table. He, Eddy, was stirring a mixture of something dark and aromatic, with a long wooden spoon in a big earthenware mixing-bowl–stirring, stirring: *Swish-wish-wish ... swish-wish-wish ...*

Swish! whispered the wooden spoon as it went round in the

bowl. *Wish! Wish!* But Eddy did not know what to wish. His not knowing made the boy at the table turn towards him; but when Eddy saw the boy's face, looked into his eyes, he knew. He knew everything, as though he were inside the boy, inside the boy's mind. He knew that this boy lived here in the basement; he was the child of the servant of the house. He helped his mother to cook the food that was put into the service-lift and hauled up to the dining-room upstairs. He helped her serve the family who ate in the dining-room, and sat at their ease in the parlour, and slept in the comfortable bedrooms above. He hated the family that had to be served. He was filled with hatred as a bottle can be filled with poison.

The boy at the table was stirring a Christmas pudding for the family upstairs, and he was stirring into it his hatred and a wish—

Wish! whispered the wooden spoon. *Wish! Wish!* And the boy at the table smiled at Eddy, a secret little smile: they were two conspirators, or one boy.

Someone screamed, and at that Eddy woke: and the screamer was Eddy himself. He tore out of his bed and his bedroom to where he could see a light in the little kitchen of the basement-flat. There were his parents, in their dressing-gowns, drinking cups of tea. The kitchen clock said nearly three o'clock in the morning.

Eddy rushed into his mother's arms with a muddled, terrified account of a nightmare about a Christmas pudding. His mother soothed him, and looked over his head to his father: 'You said it was just coincidence that neither of us could sleep tonight for bad dreams. Is Eddy part of the coincidence, too?'

Mr Napper did not answer.

Mrs Napper said: 'That hateful old corpse of a pudding, or whatever it is, isn't going to spend another minute in my home.' She set Eddy aside so that she could go to the waste-bin under the sink.

'I'll take it out,' said Mr Napper. 'I'll put it into the dustbin outside.' He was already easing his feet into his gardening shoes.

'The dustbin outside won't be cleared for another five days,' said Mrs Napper.

'Then I'll put it on the bonfire, and I'll burn it in the morning.'

'Without fail?'

'Without fail.'

Mr Napper went into the garden, carrying the Christmas

107

pudding in its newspaper wrapping; and Eddy was sent back to bed by his mother. He lay awake in bed until he heard his father's footsteps coming back from the garden and into the flat. He didn't feel safe until he had heard that.

Then he could go to sleep. But even then he slept lightly, anxiously. He heard the first of the cars in the road outside. Then he heard the people upstairs letting their dog out into the garden, as usual. The poodle went bouncing and barking away into the distance, as it always did. Then he heard his parents getting up; and then—because he wanted to see the bonfire's first burning, to *witness* it—Eddy got up, too.

So Eddy was with his father when Mr Napper went to light the bonfire. Indeed, Eddy was ahead of him on the narrow path, and he was carrying the box of matches.

'Whereabouts did you put the—the thing?' asked Eddy.

'The plum pudding? I put it on the very top of the bonfire.'

But it was not there—it had gone; there was a bit of crumpled newspaper, but no pudding. Then Eddy saw why it had gone, and where. It had been dragged down from the top of the bonfire, and now it lay on the ground, partly eaten; and beside it lay the poodle-dog from the ground floor flat. Eddy knew from the absolute stillness of the dog's body that it was dead.

Mr Napper saw what Eddy saw.

Mr Napper said: 'Don't touch the dog, Eddy. Don't touch anything. I'm going back to tell them what's happened. You can come with me.'

But Eddy stayed by the bonfire, and his father went back alone. Eddy began to shiver; he wanted to cry; he wanted to scream. He knew what he wanted to do most of all. With trembling fingers he struck a match and lit the bonfire in several places. The heap was very dry, and soon caught: it blazed merrily forming glowing caves of fire within its heart. Eddy picked up what was left of the Christmas pudding and flung it into one of the fiery caverns, and blue flames seemed to leap to welcome it and consume it.

Then Eddy began really to cry, and then felt his father's arms round him, holding him, comforting him, and heard the voice of his mother and the lamentations of the family of the ground floor flat, whose dog had been poisoned.

And the bonfire flamed and blazed with flames like the flames of Hell.

The Ivy Man

John Gordon

Three days before Christmas it began to freeze. Snow came in a thin scatter and then ceased as though it could not compete with the frost that thickened on the black trees and sparkled along the branches like a crust of diamonds.

Leo came out of the back door where the sun tried, but failed, to warm the porch. He looked up the hill to the cold rounded top where a frozen copse made a silent black explosion against the blue sky, and he muttered angrily to himself.

'I'm fed up with this weather. Why can't it snow?'

He needed snow. The grass was rimed and white, but footprints showed dark in it and whenever he tried to use his toboggan the runners grated to an uncomfortable stop.

He had gone a few paces on to the lawn, sending the greedy gulls shrieking from the scraps, when the door opened behind him and his mother appeared in the porch. She hugged herself as she felt the cold and was suddenly very girlish and so much like somebody he expected to meet soon that he blushed.

'The cold has made you very rosy,' she said. 'Where are you off to?'

'I was going to try the coomb again. It's perhaps a bit more slippery.'

The coomb was a steep fold in the hills at the other end of the village, and the best place for tobogganing.

'Oh good,' she said. 'I'd like to come with you but I've got too much to do.'

He gave her a sidelong glance.

'Now don't look at me like that,' she said. 'You know I'm busy.'

'You're scared of the coomb. I remember last year.'

'Oh am I?' She grimaced, putting the tip of her tongue out at him. 'Well you'd better get someone else to go with you.'

'I will.'

'And as you're so cocky-clever you can do something for me. Wait a minute.' She disappeared into the kitchen and came back carrying a round biscuit tin.

'What is it?'

'It's just a little Christmas cake.'

'Who for?' But he knew. She had moved so swiftly it could not have been on the spur of the moment. She had been waiting to catch him off guard.

'I made it for Mrs Cragge.' She thrust it at him so that he had to put up a hand to fend it away.

'You know I hate going there.' He refused to grasp the tin. 'Can't Dad do it?'

'He won't be home till late, you know that. And she's right by the coomb.'

There was no denying this, and the tin was pressed against his chest forcing him to make a decision. He brought his hands up and held the tin, but so lightly she could not release it.

'You know what?' he said.

'What?'

'I hate you.'

'And you are such a sweet little boy.' She kissed the air in front of his face, gave the tin a final push so that he had to clutch it or fall, and stood back smiling at him.

He tried to avoid grinning at her but could not prevent his cheeks creasing.

'What lovely dimples,' she said.

He grunted and turned to trudge up the path to the shed where he kept his toboggan.

There was not much room between the side of the house and the hedge and he could not manage to get through with toboggan and tin together, and in a spurt of temper he marched back to the shed, put the tin on a shelf inside and left it there as he clattered down the road into the village.

The runners slid quite well over the frozen green around which the cottages huddled in the bottom of the hollow, and ran smoothly on the turf path at the edge of the graveyard as he began to climb out, and when the lane dwindled into a cattle track he could hear the shouts of his friends from the still hidden coomb in the hillside. Sledging must, after all, be possible. He began to run.

On either side of the track the bare hillsides pushed the horizon half-way up the sky and he was concentrating so much on getting to the coomb he had forgotten the last cottage until a movement away to his left caught his eye. The little house was so small on the flank of the hill that it was barely visible even when he looked directly at it, but now a girl was picking her way down the crooked path from its door. There was no mistaking her; not for him. Once again, as with his mother, he blushed.

Rosy did not like him. She had resented him ever since he came to the village. It was four years since his mother and father had bought the house at the end of the street, just outside the village itself, but Rosy had never accepted him. She whispered among her friends and tried to cause trouble.

And, in return, he hated her. But he had a difficulty. No matter how hard he tried, he could not deny she was pretty. It confused him to hate her and like her at the same time.

She came closer, trying not to look at him, yet just the fact that he was there changed her expression. She sulked. It did not improve her looks but it intensified them, strengthening the already firm line of her eyebrows, darkening her already dark eyes.

'Mrs Cragge wants to see you,' said Rosy.

'Me? Are you sure?'

'It must have been you.' Suddenly she had difficulty holding back a giggle and her cheeks coloured so that, like her lips, they suited her name and she was prettier than ever.

'She doesn't want to see me,' he said. 'She didn't know I was coming this way.' Then he thought of the cake in the shed. Perhaps his mother had told her.

'She said the new boy.'

'I'm not the new boy. I've been here for years.' Rosy had succeeded in making him angry. 'She meant the other,' he said. There was a newcomer but he could not remember his name.

'No.' Rosy shook her head. 'Not him. She said the fair-haired one.' Now she was paler and suddenly seemed breathless so that her next words came out faintly and in a rush. 'She said the good-looking one.' At this, she pushed past him in the gateway and in a moment was running and stumbling across the broken ground to join the others in the coomb.

He wanted to run after her, but suddenly he felt raw and ungainly and stood where he was. And then it was too late. The

111

old woman was beckoning to him from the side of the house.

Rosy was out of sight. Leo shoved his way past the crooked gate and dragged his toboggan along the path, letting it slice its way into the ragged vegetable patch where the frost lay thick and it ran easier.

He stopped a little distance from her, not wanting to go too close. She was so old and stooped she seemed to have no shoulders. The shawl draped round her was held in place by what at first looked like a yellow brooch until he saw it was the motionless fingers of her skinny hand. And her face, too, was fixed by age, wrinkled and hardened to the bone. Her tortoise eyes barely moved.

'She ain't no good.' The old voice seemed scratchy with malice.

Leo said nothing. He clenched his jaw in anger.

'She brung me something but she ain't no good.'

'She's all right.' He could hear the fury in his tone but tried to tell himself that the old woman wasn't worth heeding. 'I like her.'

'Come you on in.' Abruptly Mrs Cragge turned her hunched back on him, not waiting to see if he would obey, and for a moment he hung back and almost left her, but then the empty doorway seemed to draw him forward and he went in to the musty, dank smell of her home.

It was dim inside, and cramped. There were so many pieces of furniture crowded into the tiny room, so many pictures hiding the walls, so many different pieces of carpet covering the floor that it was like stepping into a burrow in the hill, and the single small window looked out at the back on to the steep slope so that he could see nothing through it but frozen earth.

In an alcove was a bed, unmade, but so little disturbed that he imagined the old woman's frail bones lay on it as lightly as a bird. A small fire beneath a high, crowded mantel was almost obscured by a huge black kettle on the hob.

'She brung me them.' A yellow finger touched a pile of mince-pies on a plate. 'But she ain't no good.'

'Why?' He was glad he had left the cake at home.

'Because she's a woman, that's why.' The bent figure turned towards him. 'And it take a lad.'

'What does?'

'To save me.'

The dim light and the heavy air of the room pressed in on him.

112

He was trapped, but for what purpose he did not know. He did not reply, and she did not expect him to say anything because she had immediately turned away and shuffled round the table in the centre of the room to stand by the window. Then she beckoned to him and he threaded his way between the table and the chairs to stand alongside her.

One crooked finger pointed out of the window and up the hill and he had to stoop closer to her to see the skyline. The musty, animal smell was strong and he held his breath.

'That's where he stand,' she said. 'In that tree.'

Above them, where he knew the ground folded over the crest to dip down into the coomb, a dead tree stood alone. Its trunk was clad in a thick pelt of ivy but its straggling arms, clawing the sky, were naked and unprotected.

'I give him money to stay away.' The old woman was whispering. 'Every year I give him money. But this year he want more than that.'

'Who?' said Leo. 'Who is it?'

'Him in the tree. The one that come at Christmas.'

'Somebody threatens you?' said Leo. 'Do you mean somebody from the village?'

The old woman shook her head. 'I mean him in the tree.'

'Because, if there is anybody, I could get my Dad to do something.'

'He ain't no good.'

Leo spoke sharply, angry again. 'He'd know what to do.'

'I say he ain't no good, and he ain't! The men say they'll be here but they never come. Not one of 'em ever kept a promise. Not on Christmas Eve, not ever. So you got to do it.'

'How do you know I will?'

'Because that little maid promised that she would make you.'

He was bewildered, and his thoughts were still with Rosy when the old woman spoke again.

'He have an axe. He have a great axe, and every Christmas he stand in the tree and wait for someone to come.'

'Why?' asked Leo. 'Why does he do that?'

'His axe need blood, he say. It thirst for a Christmas sacrifice. I give him gold, I give him golden coins, but the last of my old money have gone and now he want blood.'

Leo stood back. Her mind was gone. He felt pity for her, and disgust. She was afraid for herself, believed there was an axeman

in the tree who would come for her, and yet she did not care if Leo sacrificed himself.

'You go and see him for me and I give you something,' she said.

He tried to laugh. 'But I'd be dead.'

'Young blood. True blood,' she said. 'You will have been proved.'

She was mad. 'I don't want to prove anything,' he said. 'I don't want to do it.'

'That little maid say you would.' The old woman did not look at him as she spoke.

'Did she?' he said, humouring her.

'She say that until you do she won't see you. She say she won't speak to you. She say she won't touch you until you have done that for me.'

It was like a spell and he knew that she was speaking the truth. Whatever Rosy really believed, he was certain she had entered into the old woman's ridiculous game. He made up his mind.

'All right,' he said. 'I'll see him.'

'You shall be blessed,' said the old voice seriously.

He turned and thrust his way through the door curtain and across the scullery out on to the slope. There were three days to go, so it was as good as Christmas already, and the old woman could watch as he faced the tree and proved to her there was no danger.

The cottage, with its crooked tiles and the plaster fallen off in great yellow patches, was lonely, out of sight of the village. Even the coomb, not far away, was cut off from it. The shouts of his friends did not reach him directly but echoed thinly, like ghost voices, from distant, frozen slopes. The tree, high above, reached against the sky. It was not difficult to see how it could have entered into the old woman's mind.

He climbed quickly, carrying his toboggan, and, though the air in the bottom of the valley was still, up here it began to move around him, stroking his neck with cold fingers. And it moaned through the tree as he looked up past the ivy fleece to where thin sheets of ice, teased out by the sun at noonday, hung on the undersides of the branches like blades.

The voices had gone, obliterated by the wind, and suddenly he was afraid. Yet he had to go through with it. He yelled, lifting his voice to give himself courage.

'Cut off my head if you like!' he shouted at the ivy. 'I challenge you to do it!'

He even bowed his neck to let the old woman see he shirked nothing. The wind sobbed, paused, sobbed again and then recommenced its moaning. Nothing else happened.

He raised his head, duty performed.

Now he would see Rosy.

He leant his toboggan against the ivy and took the last steps to the ridge. The slopes were useless for tobogganing but far below there was a game in progress. Rosy was there. He shouted and waved and she saw him and stood still. He began to run down to join them, but had to concentrate on keeping his feet and when he got there she was gone.

'She ran away from you,' they said. 'She doesn't want to see you.'

And it was true. He hung about close to her gate, but she did not leave home for the rest of the day. And the next day she turned and ran when he saw her in the village street. On the third day, Christmas Eve, it was even worse. They came face to face in the doorway of the village shop and for a fraction of a second he saw that she was pleased to see him, yet instantly her eyelids drooped and she went past him as though he was a stranger.

Then anger at the stupid game she was playing gripped him so ferociously that he could not tell her that he had already braved the old woman's man in the tree, and his temper came back in wave after wave throughout the day so that all the excitements of Christmas were poisoned. At home he sat at the window and watched the gulls swoop and yell in the garden, and when darkness fell he gazed beyond the glitter of the tinsel on the Christmas tree to the darkness gathered deep within it.

He went to bed, willingly and early, and for the first time in his life he did not listen to the mysterious rustlings and whispers that were excitement building up for the morning. He was far more aware of the cold bleakness of the landscape outside and his mind was wandering there as he fell asleep.

The bitter air on his cheek woke him in the middle of the night. He lay still, listening. There was no sound from downstairs. Everybody was in bed. Only the frost, tightening its grip, seemed to make the house creak. The iron barrel of the pump in the old woman's scullery would burst on a night like this.

Suddenly he sat bolt upright. The cake. The old woman's Christmas cake was still in the shed. She was alone in the hovel on the hill and he had not taken her even that single gift.

He slid out of bed. Quickly, hardly aware of what he was doing, he dressed and crept downstairs. Behind the door of the cold sitting-room he knew that parcels were piled high at the foot of the Christmas tree, but none of that was to do with him now. He found his rubber boots in the kitchen, and his coat and scarf. The lock cracked loudly as he turned the key but nothing stirred, and as he opened the door a faint light seemed to come in. He thought for a moment it was dawn, and then he saw that the air was filled with feathers of snow and the glimmer came from the soft, thick carpet that had been spread while he slept.

In the shed the cake tin was like ice. Hugging it to his chest he went down past the house to the lane. High overhead the snow swirled in the wind, but in the bottom of the valley it floated down as pure as new ash and eddied only where he disturbed the air.

There was no light in any window. It was as though every house had shut its eyes in a winter sleep. His footsteps creaking in the snow echoed faintly, almost like the sound of someone following, stealthily. Twice he stopped to search the wavering shadows behind him but nothing moved in the drifting snow. There was no sound.

He quickened his pace. The rooftops, and then the church spire, vanished behind him. Only the cottage was visible, wearing a cloak of snow.

The gate, clogged with snow, stood crookedly ajar and the vegetable patch was humped like a white sheet under which somebody was sleeping. Near the cottage the wind was moaning and lifting the top layer like smoke and pushing it against the scullery door. He had intended to leave the tin inside beside the pump, but when he lifted the latch and pushed the door it would not budge. Yet if he left the tin on the doorstep it would disappear beneath the snow.

And then it occurred to him that the window of her room would be on the sheltered side and he could leave it on the ledge where she would see it.

At the corner of the house the snow was knee-deep and he had to push his way through it to where, in the shelter of the wall, it lay thinly. The window ledge itself was almost clear, and it was broad enough to take the tin. He swept a space and put it down. He had done his Christmas duty.

He straightened, ready to turn and leave. And then, as though the ice itself had got into his bones, he was suddenly rigid. On the other side of the glass the pale curtain had moved and a face was looking directly at him. It was as lifeless as a waxwork but the eyes caught a gleam of light from the snow and pierced him. His brain refused to give him words to say and he stood where he was, caught in her spell, as a hand appeared under the face and reached towards the glass. He heard his own breath gasping inside the moan of the wind and for ten long seconds he waited to see what she would do to him. But the hand stayed where it was and he saw that it was pointing. Very slowly, painfully, he began to understand what she meant.

The tree was up there behind him and now, when Christmas was truly here, a man stood in it to threaten her. He turned. The wind spun ropes of snow up there yet the ivy fleece remained black and the branches showed up clearly in the whiteness, reaching. He looked towards her again. The pointing finger had not moved. She would not release him.

He began to climb the slope. In a few paces he was clear of the shelter of the house and the wind drove at him, caking him down one side with snow. He stumbled but kept on, higher and higher

118

towards the ridge where the branches slashed and groaned as though eager for him.

Only a tree. Yet it had the shape of a man. It was a gigantic figure in black fur of ivy, standing on the frozen ridge with its bitter axe ready to swoop with the wind and cleave his head from his body.

He wanted to whimper, but the cold was too keen for that. He wanted to turn and stumble away, but she was behind him, pointing. There was no going back. He had to put himself before the man in the tree.

Only a tree. He forced his eyes to pierce the blur of the snow and make the shape ahead of him a tree again, to make its branches spindly and dead, unable to reach for him.

He was five paces from it when the ivy coat swayed. The shape heaved its feet from the snow and lurched towards him. It came slowly, and as it did so it lifted a thick, ivy-clad arm.

Leo had time. He had time to turn and flee. He could outpace the ivy man, leaving the giant high on the hillside while he ran to the safety of the village. He knew he could do that, but at the same instant he saw what would happen if he did. He saw the great figure as it would tower over the hovel, battering at the door while the old woman crouched within.

'No!' he yelled at the top of his voice. 'No!'

The wind screamed over the ridge and rose in a roar as the arm with its vast white axe began the curve that would cleave between head and shoulder.

Still he defied it. The swing of the axe was slow as though the giant sorrowed for what he did.

Leo cried out again but the sound of his voice was lost in a scream that did not come from his own throat. And at that instant he was struck. His head jerked, and then his limbs were sprawling in the snow.

He stirred. His hand went to his neck. There was wetness. It must be blood, yet he was whole. He could sit up and gaze around. There was a figure beside him. It was no larger than himself.

'Rosy?' he said. No one else was in his mind.

She sat up, brushing snow from her face. 'I knew you would do it,' she said. 'I was watching for you.'

They were propped on their elbows, half submerged in the bed

of snow. He began to lift himself gently.

'I'm still here,' he said. 'I'm all right.'

'No you're not.' She had a handkerchief which she licked and with it rubbed his neck. 'You're bleeding.'

He pulled himself away suddenly, remembering the ivy man. The trunk of the tree lay where the wind had hurled it and its broken arm with its blade of ice was beside him.

'You pulled me back,' he said to her. 'You followed me. How did you know?'

'Old Mrs Cragge told me you'd do it. So I kept watch.'

'I thought you weren't talking to me,' he said.

Rosy got to her feet. 'I was told I could,' she said, 'when it was all over.'

They looked down towards the cottage. The curtain was back in place and all was peaceful.

'You made me face the man with the axe,' he said. 'The pair of you together. I might have been killed.'

But Rosy had left him, climbing to the crest of the slope. He waded up through the snow to be beside her. She was reaching into the broken stump of the hollow tree.

'There's nothing here,' she said. 'No golden coins.'

'Did you expect any?' he asked.

She shook her head. She was laughing. He could see the gleam of her teeth. And then, alongside her, he saw his toboggan resting against the stump where it had lain for the last three days. He looked down into the coomb. On the windward side of the hill only a thin skim of snow had settled. He hauled his toboggan free. 'It might work now,' he said.

They got astride it, facing into the teeth of the wind. He sat behind her with his arms round her and pushed off into the coomb.

The whole world tilted, the heavy sky poured past overhead, and their runners hit and lifted, jumped and jarred as the hard earth accelerated beneath them. They tossed up a spume of snow and clutched each other as the blades beneath them rocked and rang, hissed on the edge of a drift then sang on ice as, at the combe's foot, they were sent in a great curve, their runners clamouring as they gathered speed and were flung away down the track and all the way until, with the church clock sounding the hour, they came to rest in the white centre of the village where Christmas was waiting to begin.

The Christmas Gift

Hugh Oliver

It was Christmas Eve. All day it had been snowing—thick flakes
that piled against the doors and covered the fields with a carpet of
white. And in one of the lonely farmhouses on the Canadian
prairie, a child was being born.

The child's father, John, paced the floor of the living-room. He
was anxious. It was now three hours since his wife Jessie had
begun to give birth. This was to be their first child. They were
both old, and they had wanted a child for a long time.

'I wish that the doctor had been able to come,' thought John. 'If
only the snow hadn't been so deep. But what am I worrying
about? It happens to thousands every day. And Jessie's mother is
up there with her.'

Outside in the darkness, everything was silent except for the
gentle pattering of the snow flakes on the window and the trees
creaking beneath their icy loads. As John sat in front of the wood
fire, he heard a knock at the door. Imagining it might perhaps be
the doctor, he was surprised, almost fearful, to find on the step a
man he had never seen before.

'Will you give me shelter?' asked the stranger.

John hesitated. But seeing the stranger's sad appearance—snow
blanketing his coat and even clinging to his hair—he invited him in.
He helped him off with his coat, and said that he could spend the
rest of the night in front of the fire. He gave the stranger food to
eat, and the man was grateful.

'Why are you out on a snowy night like this?' asked John.

'I have much to do,' said the stranger. 'And I have far to go.'

'But where are you going?' asked John.

'In this world,' said the stranger, 'I go wherever they will
welcome me.'

John thought him odd, but questioned him no more. The
stranger warmed himself in silence for a while in front of the fire.

122

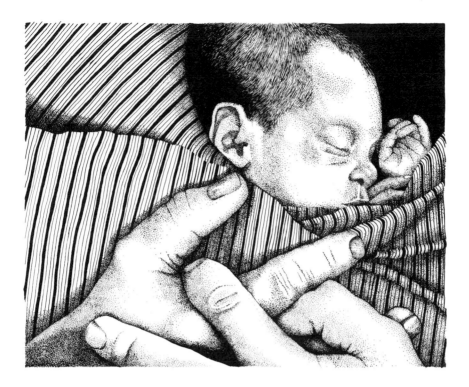

Then John told him that his wife Jessie was at that moment giving birth to their first child in the room above.

'I know,' said the stranger.

'How can you know?' asked John.

'I heard her cry out,' he said.

But John had heard no sound.

The child was born at two o'clock in the morning. It was born dead. Jessie fell into an exhausted sleep. Her mother put the dead child into the cradle beside her. Then she went downstairs to tell John what had happened.

John was numb with despair. When he looked at the table spread with all the good things for Christmas, there was no joy in him any more.

'What was it?' he asked.

'A boy,' said Jessie's mother. 'Would you like to see him?'

'I would,' answered John. 'Then I'll take him away. I shouldn't like Jessie to see him—not dead.'

John went upstairs and looked lovingly at his sleeping wife. He was thankful that she had not been taken from him as well.

He gazed at the pathetic little body in the cradle. Then he lifted it out and carried it downstairs.

He stood holding the child, and his silence was his sorrow. The stranger asked if he might take the child. Saying nothing, John gave it to him. The stranger rocked the child in his arms and kissed the child's forehead.

'Why do you do that?' asked Jessie's mother. 'The child is dead.'

'He needs to be made warm,' said the stranger.

'But he's dead,' repeated Jessie's mother.

The stranger smiled and continued to rock the child.

And John watching saw the child's eyes open, and Jessie's mother listening heard the child cry out.

'Why, you have done a miracle,' shouted John. 'You have brought the child back from death.'

'He was not dead,' said the stranger. 'He had never lived.'

He gave the child to Jessie's mother. 'Quickly!' he said. 'Take him upstairs to his mother before she wakes.' He turned to John. 'And now,' he said, 'I must be on my way.'

John did not know what to do—to laugh for joy or to weep for joy, to kiss the stranger or what to do. 'You must stay,' he said. 'You must stay with us forever.' But the stranger stood at the door putting on his coat.

'At least stay for Christmas,' pleaded John. 'Look, I have all these good things.' He pointed to the table. 'And you who have made our happiness should share it.'

But the stranger would not stay. Thanking John for his kindness, he opened the door and walked out across the snow.

It had stopped snowing. John stood at the door, watching the stranger until he was out of sight. Then, as he turned to go indoors, he was filled with wonder; for he saw that where the stranger had walked, there were no footprints in the snow.

Call me Blessed

Jacqueline Wilson

When will it be over? I had no idea it would hurt so much. I want Mother, I want Elizabeth, I want my womenfolk. I had it all planned. It was going to be so beautiful. I was going to stay calm and in control. I wasn't going to cry. I'd lie on my soft bedding in my clean little house and look at the sky through the slit of the window. I'd look up to my Lord and I'd pray to him through every pain.

I try to pray now but the pain keeps flashing through me like lightning and I can't think properly. My whispers become gasps, cries, screams. I call to the Lord because I am his chosen maiden but I can't find him. It's dark and there's just the thunder of my cries and the lightning of my pain.

I don't know what to do. I'm so scared. I didn't ever listen to the other girls when they whispered and giggled about babies. I hated that sort of sniggering. I'd walk away by myself. I'd sing to myself and dance for myself and whisper magical stories to myself. Sometimes the others would follow and make fun of me. I've never fitted in with the other villagers. I haven't any true friends, only my family. Oh Mother, I want you so. And my dear Elizabeth. How did you manage to bear this pain? Your body is becoming frail. I am young and supple and yet I can't stand it.

Oh why couldn't you wait till I was back home? Home in my house, on my soft cushions, with my womenfolk to hold my hands and sponge my face and stroke my poor swollen body. Everything is ready for you at home. There is the little cradle of twigs, the clean linen, the sweet-smelling ointments. Why are you so impatient? Why choose this filthy cave at the back of a stranger's house? The only bed is the straw, the only linen the veil from my head. Why do you want to be born in this dark and lonely place reeking of animal dung?

The cattle munch and murmur, oblivious, but my own little ass lifts its head and brays uneasily as if it's in pain too. It's lame after the long journey. Oh, that endless trek through Samaria, the sharp bones of the little ass chafing my thighs, the dust coating my skin, lining my garments, the tension turning every muscle into a sharp stone. I got so unbearably stiff that I slid down from the ass and tried to walk but I couldn't cope with the clumsiness of my body. I wanted to run like the wind but I could only shamble like a beggar. I had to be helped back on to the little ass, weak and sweating, the pains already flickering in my stomach and spine.

I didn't dare acknowledge them. I stayed silent all that last dusty day. I bent my head so that the pain wouldn't show on my face. I knew it was too soon, I knew I'd have no-one to help me, I knew it was a nightmare when I so wanted it to be like a golden dream. Like my golden dream of Gabriel. The golden voice, the golden heat, the brush of golden wings, and then the golden trumpets inside my head proclaiming my awesome gift from God. I heard the glory of those golden trumpets throughout these last long months. They blared out triumphantly, so that I need not listen to the whispers, the comments, the jeers. They laughed in the village. Some said I was mad, that I'd always talked to myself and that was a certain sign. Some said I was bad, that I'd lain with other men and should now be tested with the bitter waters. And Joseph said . . .

Sometimes the trumpets were not quite loud enough. I could hear Joseph's words, I could see his anguish and shame. Some said he should spurn me, some said he should stone me. But he stood up with me in front of all the villagers and he married me, even though he knew I was carrying a child that wasn't his.

'A golden child. God's only son. He chose me, Joseph. An angel came down from Heaven and seared me with the golden spirit and now I have God's golden child within me.' I whispered on our wedding night, going down on my knees to Joseph to make him understand. But he couldn't hear the trumpets even though my head rang with their golden harmonies. He turned away from me. He did not lie with me even on our wedding night. He has barely touched me since. His face looks as if it's carved from a rock. But his eyes watch me. They follow me all the time. They are red with anger and grief, although he never lets me see the tears spill. I want to ease his pain but he will not let me be close to him. He is a rock man, hard and unyielding. He has left me now, in my lonely

agony. He is out walking in the dark while I writhe here in the straw.

'Joseph, for pity's sake, come to me!'

I call again and again. I call until my voice is hoarse. And then I hear a rustle in the straw, sense a large shape above me, smell the faint scent of sycamore clinging to his clothing. He crouches beside me. There's a lull between the lightning and I struggle to sit up, to see his face in the murk of the moonlight. I see the salt glitter on his cheeks.

'Don't hate me, husband,' I gasp.

'I don't hate you, Mary. I've tried to hate you but I love you too much. I've loved you since you were a small girl skipping past my shop. Remember, I pinned a few wood-shavings in your hair for fancy curls. You looked so shy and solemn at first but then you saw your shadow in the sunlight and you smiled at your silly curls. That smile stirred strong feelings in my heart. I knew then that all I wanted in the whole world was to make you my wife. I am your husband now but I am helpless. I don't know what to do for you. I can't bear to see you struggling like this.'

'Stay with me. Please stay with me.'

The lightning strikes and I scream and flail my arms and he catches hold of me, gripping with his strong hands until the flashing is finished.

'I'll stay with you,' Joseph whispers into the darkness. 'You are my wife and I am your husband. I will stay.'

I have lived as a maiden since my marriage but now the storm in my body blows away all my modesty. I forget I'm me, Mary. I am part of the storm, the bellow of thunder, the flash of lightning, and I rage. I am torn one way, torn another, torn until I am suddenly, shockingly split into two. Two people. I am one and you are the other. Still joined but separate. The storm is over.

I reach down and hold you in my hands. I stare at you in wonder. I stare at the bloom of your cheeks, pink as pomegranates. I stare at the milky paleness of your tiny wrists, the spiderweb delicacy of your veins. I lay you on my head-dress but before I swaddle you I want to worship you. I rub my cheek against the damp tendrils of your hair. I kiss one tiny curled foot. I touch one small clenching fist and it fastens round my finger. There is no doubt now. You are my golden gift from God.

I wrap you up reverently, my hands trembling. I hold you in my arms and shudder as one more lightning flicker contracts my womb. In that searing second I see myself still holding you in my arms when you're a grown man. A golden grown man and yet you seem as stiff and still as a babe in swaddling clothes. Tears stream from my eyes although I don't understand.

'Don't cry, my sweet little wife,' Joseph whispers, and he kisses my eyes. 'The pain is all over now.'

But I know it is only just beginning.

The Christmas Present

Kathleen Hersom

I thought there could be nothing easier than writing a Christmas story. There would be no need to rack my brains for a plot, or struggle to create life-like characters. I would simply put down on paper that story which floats into my head each year during the second half of December. It comes as regularly as the mince pies and the plum pudding and the carols. For years I had intended writing it down. Once I put my hand to the pen, I was sure there would be no trouble.

So I rollicked away into the first paragraph, describing a horde of children plodging through the snow in a deep forest; six inches deep, at least, that snow was, and the children, muffled from top to toe, cherry-nosed and eyes shining, were carrying lanterns. Branches heavy with snow bent down to touch them, and a million stars sparkled in the frosty sky. It was almost midnight, and I think the bells were ringing. They made their way to the little church conveniently situated in a forest clearing, where midnight mass was to be celebrated. Just like the Christmas cards it was, the roof smothered in deep snow overhanging into icicles, the dark trees behind it, light piercing from the windows, and small footprints smudging through the snow up to its door. The children left their lanterns and their snowballs in the porch and hurried inside, almost filling the church. A few small square women sat at the back, their heads swathed in white medieval-looking wimples. A tiny boy swung a censer, while a great genial priest loomed over him. And through the little window above the altar one big star outshone all the rest.

When the mass was over and the children had crossed themselves for the last time, they picked up their lanterns and tugged me by the hand to the little wooden house in the forest where they all lived together, and where they had invited me to a party that was to start at three o'clock in the morning.

Their home inside was scrubbed and neat, and all the rafters and most of the walls were covered with sweet-smelling fir-branches; gingerbread-men and star biscuits hung from the beams, and there were red and white decorations, and flags. Trestle-tables set for some kind of feast were on three sides of the room, and everywhere there was bustle and activity, something like one of those pictures by Breughel, but not so much food.

Here I broke off to read back what I had written so far. The way I had written it made me feel uncomfortable. Where on earth had all this phoncy icing-sugar fantasy come from? Was it a nostalgic travesty of the Grimms' fairy stories that had been told to me so often in childhood, translated, perhaps, into a more recent Disneyism? I had intended surging on to the end before making any alterations, but now I felt compelled to go back and get my feet planted firmly on the ground before drowning in a sea of whimsy, and take out all that Snow Whiteish stuff straight away.

But that wasn't easy. Implausible it might be, but could it be called phoney once I accepted that, after all, it wasn't fiction I was writing? It wasn't fiction because it had all really happened and I had been at the party myself, and in that snow, and at the church, so I knew every word was authentic.

The forest I had described was the Duisburger Wald; a great welcome stretch of green in the industrial Ruhr valley. The time was the night of December 24-25, 1946. The children carrying their lanterns through the snow were all Displaced Persons, lost Polish children who had become separated from their parents during the course of the war, or in the confusion and upheaval that followed the ending of it. They did not live in the usual prefabricated sprawl of D.P. camps that littered Germany at that time, but in a small wooden chalet that had once been used for

132

some week-end forestry activity by the Hitler Youth. With them were a few Polish women separated from their own families, all looked after by a kindly housemother.

I had described them, accurately enough, as 'muffled from head to toe': army greatcoats cut down to size (or, more often, not cut down to size) are all-enveloping. Even an old battledress will reach to the toes provided you are small enough to start with. And whose nose would not be red on a night as cold as that one was? Torches might have been more likely than those over-picturesque Dickensian lanterns, but batteries were unobtainable, so it was lanterns that lighted them through the forest to the midnight mass–though I never learned how they came by those lanterns.

The D.P.s had a wonderful knack of 'organizing' things, especially for celebrations. The exuberance of snow and frost and icicles was no Christmas-card make-believe, but just as I said. Old meteorological records somewhere would bear me out. True, I hadn't actually counted the stars, but I remember looking up and thinking that a million was about what it looked like. I could cut out the ringing bells in my final draft. I think they really were there, but so many bells had been melted down for the German war effort that they might just possibly have been a wishfully imagined recollection.

I moved on to what I had written about the midnight mass. Not being a Catholic I was wary of much detailed description here for fear of missing the right significances, but I firmly crossed out that great star looking through the window. Even in 1946 I thought it too trite and dramatic to be true–although it really was there. I let the incense stay, although I remember now that it too had been unobtainable at the time–that jovial Santa-Claus-cum-Friar-Tuck-like-priest was an unscrupulous old bounder when it came to obtaining the unobtainable–and I liked the smell. Good smells were important in those hungry days when the smell of watery turnip soup seeped out of every kitchen, and the stink of corruption hung around the uncleared rubble that stretched for scores of miles beyond the forest.

I carried on with my story, reporting, not imagining, that three-o'clock-in-the-morning party where I had been a guest.

'The children who were too young to have been to mass had been shaken awake and carried in, wrapped in grey army blankets, to blink at the precious candles — candles whose burning was so carefully rationed and conserved — and to poke inquisitive hopeful fingers at the one-inch squares of chocolate set singly at each place. It was good that on this occasion at least, it would not be syphoned off on to the black market.

'The party was a double celebration: not only for Christmas, but for the reunion of one of the Polish women with her children from whom she had been separated for more than four years. Her sixteen-year-old daughter, trailing a small staircase of younger brothers and sisters, had somehow floundered her way across Germany from the east, without documents, and although transport had been almost non-existent. They had arrived

eventually, on this Christmas Eve, at this small Polish barrack in the Duisburger Wald, where, unknown to them, their mother was living.'

How the red tape of occupying armies, the regulations of Military Government and its Control Commission, the ministrations of the Red Cross and UNRRA had been dodged or overcome, or just ignored, I cannot now remember, if I ever heard. Nor did I know how long they had been on their way. That did not matter. With a good map of Germany and Poland, and reference to a history of the Second World War, I might lapse into real fiction here. This is where I might start imagining some of the dangers, narrow escapes, blind eyes and helping hands that there must have been on their road. There could certainly be more than just one story here.

It was, indeed, a well of material to draw on for stories; a remarkable, courageous journey, but not without parallel. I had read articles about similar triumphs written shortly after the war, and I saw a film once that reminded me of it. But never since that night have I been asked to believe such an audacious coincidence as those real children's dramatic entry on Christmas Eve, spotlighted against the background of evergreens and snow and frost and red and white paper flowers and makeshift Polish flags. No short story could hold it.

I was sure that no editor nowadays would find that absurdly neat old-fashioned happy ending acceptable. It was so unlikely that Stanislava and the other children would find their mother at all, but to find her on Christmas Eve of all the three hundred and sixty-five possible days was timing that was far too contrived to be credible–how could I convince anyone that it was not 'contrived' because there was not a single invention in it? Improbable facts make impossible fiction.

Perhaps as a *story* it would be better if I could postpone their arrival till the spring. It would be years before all the Poles would be able to leave Germany. There was no hurry. Spring would thaw out all that excessive snow and frost, and extinguish the spluttering candles and the lanterns at one stroke. There would be no need or reason for the midnight mass. It would perhaps be better artistically that way, as well as easier to believe.

But I braked again. That wouldn't be a Christmas story any

more, and it was a Christmas story I was supposed to be writing. A story that wasn't a Christmas story would have no place in this book.

So that is where I left my Christmas story, with that celebration party of a displaced family in the heart of a German forest; with bright beady eyes in Slavonic faces watching a mother enjoying the best Christmas present she could ever wish to have. The facts are so improbable that it would certainly have made impossible fiction. But that doesn't matter, because, as I said before, it is not fiction that I have been writing, whatever the editor, or the readers and I were expecting. The 'story' that floats into my head every Christmas really happened, nearly forty years ago, just exactly as I have written it.

Call it reminiscence, or even history, if you must have a label. It is certainly not fiction.

Get Lost

Robin Klein

'Just relax, dear,' they said, and his mind, groping up from under the anaesthetic snarled, 'Why the hell should I?' But the nurse didn't hear more than a sigh of pain and protest. Trained, capable hands ministered to his pain. Objects swam like street lights seen through mist, and when the mist shifted, he saw that they were kind faces framed in white veils. Brad didn't pay any attention to the kindness, even when the mist cleared altogether.

'Knocked yourself about a bit, haven't you?' said Sister Hallam. 'It's a shame, right at the start of the Christmas holidays.'

Get lost, Brad thought. He stared past her at a little boy sitting up in a cot like a seal pup on an ice floe. 'Hey, kid!' he hissed. 'Quit gawking or I'll come over there and land you one.' He scowled ferociously, and the little kid bawled, and Brad felt satisfied.

Someone oughta bawl about this pain, he thought irritably, locked into his aching, battered body. Sister Hallam plucked the little boy out of his cot and comforted his wails against her blue uniform. She looked at Brad with astonishment.

'Shove his cot out on the freeway,' Brad said.

'I like polite people in this ward, young man,' she said sharply. 'I don't stand for any nonsense whatsoever.' She gave the little boy a matchbox tractor and set him back in the cot. Then she fixed Brad's pillows so he'd know that, although she didn't hold with any nonsense, she understood about pain. Brad deliberately used the arm that wasn't in plaster to shove the pillows back the way they'd been. The effort was like barbed wire, but he didn't allow his face to register anguish.

'For a boy who came off second best to a horse, you've got a lot to learn about various things,' Sister Hallam said. 'There are two little words called "thank you", for a start.'

Brad frowned savagely, and the frown was like hornets trapped behind his eyebrows. There was scarcely a part of him that didn't hurt. The horse, he thought, remembering. It shied at the big black snake curling up from nowhere, and I got dumped and went for a sixer over the gully. Spooky beggar, that horse.

His mind veered from the memory, but he forced it back, looking at the fall impersonally, as though it were television. He watched this skinny kid crashing down onto rocks, and felt nothing. Then the nothing stopped, in spite of his formidable will power, and he began to shake all over.

How long had he lain there, shattered, before they came? Flies and vomit all over his face, and the summer sun like a mad crazy thing whirling across the sky. They didn't even miss him at the house, not for hours. His uncle's voice: 'What's that bloody useless kid done now? Ambulance job, and God, look at the busted reins, someone get that bridle off, more bloody expense!'

His Aunty Joyce climbed down with the first-aid box from the ute, and his cousins' faces were a blur across the rim of the gully. 'Rack off!' he yelled, seeing them as sinister Jack o'Lantern pumpkins, and his aunt said, 'Even if you are hurt, don't you dare talk to the girls like that!' Dislike, nudging at hatred in her eyes, and he would have given her cheek, but his uncle came back, and he was scared of that dour, powerful man. So he'd shut up and dealt with the pain and fear in other ways.

There had been a bird, like a silver dart cleaving the sky from one horizon to the other. Be all right, he thought, having wings. He flew with the bird, inside his mind, up there where it was clean and safe and not cluttered up with the human race.

'You behave yourself in that Langmong hospital,' his aunt said. 'Don't you give them nurses no trouble. Maybe your Aunty Pat might stir herself and get in to visit you, that side of town. I can't leave the baby.'

She didn't kiss him goodbye, and Brad wouldn't have known how to handle it if she'd tried. He was too busy, anyhow, keeping his face like a mask as they moved him onto the stretcher, and the stretcher into the ambulance. He wanted to scream, but you didn't ever let people see how it was with you.

The ambulance man, the one who stayed in the back with him, was genial and kind. 'Long ride to Langmong, mate,' he said. 'Least you didn't bust your skull. Busted just about everything else, but if the old skull's apples, nothing to worry about, eh?'

'Who's worried?' Brad said sullenly, and turned his face to the window.

'Who's worried?' he snarled, every time they told him with false jauntiness at the hospital that they were just taking him down to X-Ray, just changing a dressing, that the doctor wanted to have another look at him.

Did he want something to read, Sister Hallam asked. If he liked, Jimmy from the end bed would come and sit with him, and they could play Monopoly.

'Get lost!' Brad yelled, and she stopped being so nice. He shut himself away while she was telling him off, and telling the other nurses at the desk what a pill he was. He didn't care one way or another what they thought. The conversation at the desk was what he'd been hearing as a background all his life. What a pill he was, what a pain.

He watched an aeroplane in the square of sky caught by the window. A big jet, like an eagle, riding the air up there. Be OK, he thought, being a pilot. Maybe not on a jet, too many bloody people to cart around, but on one of those little private planes, that'd be OK, a job like that. Just you, airborne, miraculously grown wings. You could get right up there and not have to listen to anyone, not have to look at anyone. Best of all would be if you could find a hole in the sky and zip through it and never come back.

139

'Let's get you tidied up for visiting hour, love,' someone said. 'I'm Nurse Griggs, the nursing aide for this ward.'

Face like a midsummer moon, faint moustache, an apron straining across great breasts, strong hands, voice like gravel crashing out of a truck. Strewth! Brad thought. Where did they dig you up from?

'I'm on Sister Thing's list,' he said sourly.

'Not any more. Ward's too busy. I've been sent over from Four West to lend a hand.'

Hand, he thought. Bloody shovel!

She shovelled him easily from one side of the bed to the other with her big gentle hands, washing the bits of him that weren't in plaster or bandaged. Her wedding ring was embedded in rolls of fat, like a forgotten plant nursery label still attached to a bough. Wedding ring, he thought, sneering. How'd she ever land anyone, looking like that?

'You aren't helping me any, laying there like a hunk of concrete,' she said placidly. 'Anyone would reckon you had a busted leg and a busted arm and some ribs gone on strike. Where's your clean pj's?'

'How the hell should I know?'

Nurse Griggs looked in the empty locker and then went along to the ward cupboard and got a pair from there. Brad was sweaty with embarrassment while she changed him into the clean pyjamas, though the embarrassment, when it travelled as far as his eyes, glinted out coldly as hatred. 'I can do that,' he barked. 'I ain't no cripple.'

She watched him fumble, left handed. She had nice eyes, the colour of faded jeans, and her mouth in that uncomely face was pleasant to look at. Brad didn't deign to look at her at all.

'I fell off a horse once,' she said. 'Only I never did it right on Christmas.'

'I don't mind being stuck here for Christmas,' he said aggressively. 'Don't make no difference. Me Dad'll bring me a model aeroplane kit. Always does, every Christmas. Got a whole room full at home.'

'They're beaut, those model kits. I like to see kids make up things like that, instead of glued to the telly all the time. Your Dad coming in tonight?'

'Mind your own business,' Brad said.

My Dad, he thought, lying in his fresh bed in hospital pyjamas, clean and despairing. Me old man. Jesus, don't even know who he is, or what he looks like. Never seen him, and don't care, anyhow.

He lay, not caring, suffering, through the visiting hour. Jimmy's parents came and brought him one of those battery-operated computer games. Big deal. Rob's Mum came and read him a book. Everyone's parents and aunts and uncles and cousins came, and each bed was fringed with a circle of visitors, and his was a deserted island in that busy ocean. He shut his eyes and pretended to be dead. When Nurse Griggs came with cocoa and biscuits he muttered, 'Take that muck away. Cocoa here tastes like pee.'

'Lovely talk that is, right on Christmas.'

'Christmas can get stuffed.'

'Brad the bad lad,' she said, helping herself to the biscuits he chose not to eat. 'Brad the cad.'

'Get lost.'

'I'm never lost. Always know exactly where I'm going, and right now it's taking these tired old feet off this ward and home. You're a right old misery guts, aren't you? I reckon they ought to bung you over in the old men's ward.'

'Wouldn't be any worse than this crummy one.'

Nurse Griggs straightened his blankets. She glanced at his clenched hands and unfolded his fingers one by one and laid his hands gently on the turned-down sheet. Then she switched off the bedlamp and went away.

During the night he had such pain that he almost rang the buzzer and asked for help. His extravagant pride ruled that out. He stared into the darkness of the ward and thought desperately of wings. The flying foxes skimming down at dusk into the Moreton Bay fig tree at the farm—they looked beautiful in flight, but when they scrabbled about in the tree, they were ugly, tattered umbrellas. He felt like a broken umbrella himself, imagining his shattered bones as the broken ribs of an old umbrella. His skin felt as susceptible as ripped silk. He explored his lacerated face with the fingers of his good hand, whimpering, but when the night sister came to his bed, he pretended to be asleep. 'You OK, dear?' she whispered. 'Need anything?'

Wings, he beseeched her, imploring, without making any sound at all.

'Get lost,' he mumbled aloud.

In the morning Nurse Griggs brought in a Christmas tree and set it at the end of the ward. She was clumsy and dropped things, and had difficulty threading the silver ornaments. The sister, behind her back, secretly re-arranged the decorations more artistically. Bloody great galah, Brad thought. Clumsy fat drip.

'Where are you going for Christmas, Griggs?' the junior nurse asked while they made his bed.

'Not going anywhere,' Nurse Griggs said. 'Funny how I always cop that Christmas roster, every year without fail.'

'Very funny,' the junior nurse said. She was practising to top the state list when she graduated, and she smiled tenderly at Brad. Would he like some magazines, a crossword puzzle book, some more orange juice? Her cultivated tenderness was all wasted on Brad. He deliberately knocked over the jug of orange juice and told her to get lost. The ward sister came and ticked him off, but he stared coldly past their anger at the sky. A summer sky, so intensely blue that it hurt your eyes to look.

'Pity you didn't have your new aeroplane kit right now,' said Nurse Griggs while she cleaned up the mess. 'Keep you out of strife. When did your old man say he was bringing it in?'

'Tonight maybe. He can't always make it. He's a test pilot, see.'

'I might ask him to fly you up to the moon and leave you there,' said Nurse Griggs. 'You could chuck all the orange juice you like around up there. With the air force, is he, your Dad?'

'He's a wing commander. Might get him to drop a few bombs on this dump. Drop them on that Sister Whatsit.'

'Your models must look a treat, with him to help you make them up. You're a lucky bloke. What kinds have you got so far?'

Brad glared at her bleakly. He'd never in his life had pocket money, never in his life been into a shop that sold model kits. 'Hundreds,' he said. 'Got 'em all threaded up on the ceiling.'

'Your room must look fantastic. If a breeze came, all those little planes would look as though they were flying.'

He thought of the corner of the veranda at the farm where he slept; the spare corners of other people's lives and houses where he had grown up, passed from corner to corner, house to house. You be a good boy at your Aunty Joyce's; we'll maybe have you back here for the winter, but I'm not making any promises.

Only try and get lost somewhere on the way, Brad, it's more convenient.

143

'Yeah,' he said indifferently. 'My room's fantastic. Ceiling's all painted over blue, so it looks like the sky. Me old man thought of that, when we were hanging up all them planes.'

He watched paper forests of Christmas cards grow on everyone's lockers. Nurse Griggs hung up streamers where they got in everyone's way and when she was off duty, Sister Hallam moved them to different places. Each day during the visiting hour, while cicadas shrilled against the screened windows, he hunched himself in a pretence of sleep, and thought of the letters and telephone calls that must be circulating on his account. You'll have to have him for a bit, Pat, when he comes out of that hospital. I've got the baby. I can't be running around after him. I had him all the last school holidays, anyhow. Let's say we ask Laurie, then, if he can go up there. About time they pulled their weight.

Each day Nurse Griggs wiped down his bare and empty locker without comment, and fetched another pair of hospital pyjamas from the ward cupboard.

One night, when she was on late shift, and his leg hurt so badly that he wept, raging at himself, she sat comfortably by his bed in the circle of light from his bedlamp, and held his hand. Brad was

144

hardly aware of it; if he had been, he would have snatched his hand away immediately. That day they had done something to his leg in the operating theatre. Under the dressing it hurt unbearably, which was a stupid, lying, cheating word, he thought. Unbearable. When you had no choice but to endure.

'They can't give you any more stuff for the pain just yet, love,' Nurse Griggs said. 'I'm sorry.' Brad clung to her strong hand like someone being hoisted into a lifeboat.

'I never asked, even,' he snarled. 'I'm OK. Go and drive someone else batty, you old cow. Dunno what you're hanging around for.'

'Short staffed, that's why you're seeing so much of me. Always short staffed at Christmas. That's why I've bagged this chair of yours, to get the weight off my feet a bit. My word, Christmas, I'm worn out. Double shift they'll be asking me to do next, I shouldn't wonder. They'll give your Dad time off for Christmas, won't they, to come and see you in hospital? Where's he stationed, anyhow?'

'North Pole,' Brad said harshly. He was looking at the stars caught in the window frame. Be OK, he thought, to have wings and get that far away, up among those brilliant, distant worlds. No hassles up there, everything all clean and quiet and empty.

'Got a jet plane like an eagle,' he whispered into the pillow. 'Got a rocket, and one of them World War One planes with the double wings. You should see them. Got them all hung up in my room at home, thousands of them. When there's a breeze, they all look like they're flying.'

'You're a lucky boy,' Nurse Griggs said gently, and in his despair he clung so hard that the wedding ring seared into her flesh, but she didn't take her hand away.

On Christmas day the visiting hour lasted all afternoon. Brad ignored all those people who approached and tried to draw him into things, and his face was hard and forbidding. 'Let me help you sit up so you can see Santa Claus,' the junior nurse coaxed.

Brad took one look, then lay flat and pulled the bedclothes up to his chin, wanting no part of it. It was their stupid make-believe world, not his. A great lumbering Santa Claus in plastic boots any fool could see were just plain ordinary gum boots. Ringing a stupid bell. 'Get lost!' he hissed when the Santa Claus put a box, wrapped in bright paper, on the end of his bed. He pretended it

145

wasn't there. The other kids were given presents, all the same, all books. He shut his eyes and kept them shut until all the visitors left and it was evening.

Didn't even take her wedding ring off, he thought sourly. Santa Claus a sheila with a wedding ring, huh!

The big box weighed down the blankets at the end of his bed. Some nurse, he thought, bunging things down on people's gammy legs, wonder they don't give her the sack.

When the ward routine was at its busiest and he knew he could do so without being noticed, he opened the box and looked at the beautiful model plane kit, which must have cost someone a good deal of money. His face didn't allow itself any change of expression.

Nurse Griggs came singing down the ward with her raspy tin-bucket voice. She whipped the spreads from each bed as she passed and folded them over the bed rails. She seemed to have as many arms as a signpost, he thought. A ruddy great signpost right there in the middle of the ward.

'Look lively,' she said, attending briskly to his bed. 'Lights out soon. And do me a favour, seeing it's Christmas, how about you don't tell me to get lost, just for once?'

But Brad was looking at his plane. He ran his fingertips over the various sections, like a blind person learning to read braille. One day I'll get a real one, he thought. You wait and see, Griggs. I'll come back here and take you up for a ride on your day off. Just you and me.

'Lost your tongue?' Nurse Griggs asked. 'Cat got it, maybe?'

'I'm not lost,' Brad said. 'I'm right here.'

A Present for Grannie Fox

Norman Smithson

Couldn't think of anything until Christmas Eve night. Jibs came on the paper round with me and Tommy Haircuts. After we'd finished, Tommy gave me one-and-a-tanner from his tips. Didn't tell me how much he got altogether. Think it was about ten bob.

'Don't spend it all at once.'

Then Tommy jumped on his bike, speeded off down the street. Me and Jibs set off walking.

'What are you going to buy Grannie Fox for Chrissy then?'

'Nowt. I don't think.'

'You'll have to buy her summat.'

'Why?'

'Because you will.'

Came to Dalby's shop window. Stopped. Had a look. It was all done up with trimmings and fairy lights. It was full of stuff. Big boxes of chocolates and spice and books and cigars and toys.

'Don't know what to buy.'

Our breath frosted up on the window. Stamped our feet, blew on our hands to keep warm.

'Why don't you buy her a cigar?'

'Don't think she likes them. She only smokes a pipe.'

'Oh.'

Blew on his hands, put them round his red nose, try to warm it up a bit.

'I bet she does smoke a cigar—at Christmas.'

'D'yer think so?'

'Yes. Everybody smokes cigars at Christmas.'

He thought for a minute.

'Look. I know. Why don't you buy her some chocolates and a cigar as well.'

'Will I have enough money?'

Couldn't reckon-up the money. But Jibs could. He was good at that.

'Yes, course you will. If you get a sixpenny cigar, and a sixpenny box of chocolates, that's tenpence ha'penny. So you'll have...'

Scratched the back of his nut.

'...you'll have sempence-ha'penny left.'

That sounded all right. Only fivepence at the pictures tonight. Still have something left, go shares for five cigs. No good buying anything for my dad, because he'd most likely be bringing me something. In any case, got more money than us. Went in the shop. Asked Old Man Dalby for a sixpenny cigar.

'Who's it for?'

'Grannie Fox.'

'For who?'

'Grannie Fox.'

'Oh.'

Looked at me, a bit queer. Thought I'd better tell him.

'She only smokes a pipe really, 'cept at Christmas.'

'Oh, well make sure you give it to her then.'

Gave me a cigar wrapped in silver paper. Then, got a box of chocolates. Wrapped it up in fancy paper. Just as I was going out, Jibs put his head round the door. Shouted out to Old Man Dalby:

'Got any Wild Woodbines, mister?'

'Yes, lad, we have.'

'Well tame 'em then. Ha-ha, ha-ha.'

Dashed out, ran off. Then stopped to look in all the other shop windows. All lit up by this time, same as the buses, cars, speeding up and down Woodlestown Street. First window we passed, the tripe shop. But nobody was buying any. Didn't blame them either. Who wanted tripe at Christmas! Except maybe Willie J. He was mad on tripe, done up with milk and onions. Next window we came to was Brown's Pork Shop. Full of bacon, pork, stuff like that. And piled up in one corner, dirty-big meat pies, big as footballs. Tommy Haircuts says they make them from dead cats and dogs, after they've been put through the mincer.

'What are you having for your Christmas dinner?'

'Piece of pork, I think. An plum pudden, and rum sauce.'

'We're having a turkey, man. I'm having a leg to messen.'

'I bet you never scoff it all.'

'Bet I do, man.'

'Bet you don't, man.'

'Bet I do, man.'

'Bet you don't, man.'

'Bet I do, man.'

Biggest romancer under the sun, Jibs was, at times.

Next shop we saw was the chemist's. Mrs Thingy's favourite. But there was nothing to see there, except pills and brush and comb sets and soap. So, skipped that. Went to Slaters. That was just as bad. All they sold there, Sunday clothes, like ties and socks.

'My auntie Bessie allus buys me ties and socks.'

'Yer. Can buy them any time.'

Now, ran over to Chas. Ford's, the toy shop. Best window we'd seen so far. All crinkly with trimmings and lights. Full of things like forts, soldiers, garages, farm yards.

Next, passed Jones and Jones, the suit shop, where we took club tickets for new pants and windjammers. Me and Jibs just looked at the football jerseys, then nipped across the road, between the buses, to the butcher's. There, massive sides of meat, hung up on big hooks, inside the window. And smaller lumps of deep red meat, and chickens, sausages, pig's trotters, black puddings, laid out on the white marble slab. While we were looking, one of the butchers came out with a sweeping brush. Blood on his blue and white striped apron. His face, red as a tomato, from eating too much raw meat. Had a thick mop of black hair, like Tarzan's.

'Nar then, me lucky lads. Mind out o't way a minute while I sweep up.'

Pushed my arm to move me. Box of chocolates I was holding caught the top of my leg, went flying out of my hands. Landed on the causer-edge. Slithered over on to the iron fever grating. Slipped through one of the holes. Oh heck. Flipping heck.

'Hey, look what you've done now.'

Ran over to the fever grate. Looked down it. One of them right deep grates, leads to the sewers.

'Never get that back now. Still, you've got a cigar, so it doesn't matter all that much.'

Just stood looking down the grate. Thinking about all the money, spent for nowt. Then Tarzan came over. Jibs told him all about what I'd bought it for. Laid it on a bit. Then Tarzan slapped me on the back.

'Never mind, lad. Let's see if we can find something else for Grannie Fox.'

Took us into the shop. Started to wrap up a big string of sausages. Another butcher came out of the back room. Must have been the boss because he had a bald head, wore glasses. Tarzan told him what had happened. The boss butcher laughed his hat off. Shoved more sausages on the pile, wrapped them.

'There you are, lad. Take them home for Grannie Fox.'

'He's only got sempence-ha-penny.'

Showed the boss butcher my money.

'Don't want any money, lad.'

'Don't you?'

'No.'

'Right. Ta.'

Wondered what was up with him. Mrs Thingy said they were daylight robbers, some of the poor meat they'd had, lately.

'Tarrah.'

'Tarrah.'

Soon as we were outside, Jibs scooted off. Said he had to see somebody. I walked on to our street, feeling dead chuffed. Got inside, Grannie Fox pointed.

'What have you got there?'

Perhaps she thought I'd knocked it off.

'Some sausages and a cigar for your Christmas present.'

'Some what?'

Told her again.

'Oh.'

Then she wanted to know where I'd got the money from. All the details. Told her all about it.

'I thought I told you to keep away from that Tommy Haircuts.'

Lucky for me, she didn't bother any more, and we had some of the sausages for our tea. Then sat smoking her cigar. After a few puffs, she seemed very pleased. Smiled:

'Here you are.'

Gave me sixpence.

'Get off to the pictures with you.'

So I did, and got five cigs on my own, without having to go shares with anybody.

Adrian Mole's Christmas

Sue Townsend

Saturday December 19th

I've got no money for Christmas presents. But I have made my
Christmas list in case I find ten pounds in the street.

> Pandora–Big bottle of Chanel No. 5 (£1.50)
> Mother–Egg-timer (75p)
> Father–Bookmark (38p)
> Grandma–Packet of J cloths (45p)
> Dog–Dog chocolates (45p)
> Bert–20 Woodbines (95p)
> Auntie Susan–Tin of Nivea (60p)
> Sabre–Box of Bob Martins, small (39p)
> Nigel–Family box of Maltesers (34p)
> Miss Elf–Oven-glove (home-made)

Wednesday December 23rd

9a.m. Only two shopping days left for Christmas and I am still
penniless. I have made a Blue Peter oven-glove for Miss Elf, but in
order to give it to her in time for Christmas I will have to go into
the ghetto and risk getting mugged.

I will have to go out carol singing, there is nothing else I can do
to raise finance.

10p.m. Just got back from carol singing. The suburban houses
were a dead loss. People shouted, 'Come back at Christmas',
without even opening the door. My most appreciative audience
were the drunks staggering in and out of the Black Bull. Some of
them wept openly at the beauty of my solo rendition of 'Silent
Night'. I must say that I presented a touching picture as I stood in
the snow with my young face lifted to the heavens ignoring the
scenes of drunken revelry around me.

I made £3.13½ plus an Irish tenpence and a Guinness bottletop. I'm going out again tomorrow. I will wear my school uniform, it should be worth a few extra quid.

Thursday December 24th

Took Bert's Woodbines round to the home. Bert is hurt because I haven't been to see him. He said he didn't want to spend Christmas with a lot of malicious old women. Him and Queenie are causing a scandal. They are unofficially engaged. They have got their names on the same ashtray. I have invited Bert and Queenie for Christmas Day. My mother doesn't know yet but I'm sure she won't mind, we have got a big turkey. I sang a few carols for the old ladies. I made two pounds eleven pence out of them so I went to Woolworth's to buy Pandora's Chanel No. 5. They hadn't got any so I bought her an underarm deodorant instead.

The house looks dead clean and sparkling, there is a magic smell of cooking and satsumas in the air. I have searched around for my presents but they are not in the usual places. I want a racing bike, nothing else will please me. It's time I was independently mobile.
11p.m. Just got back from the Black Bull. Pandora came with me, we wore our school uniforms and reminded all the drunks of their own children. They coughed up conscience money to the tune of twelve pounds fifty-seven! So we are going to see a pantomime on Boxing Day and we will have a family bar of Cadbury's Dairy Milk each!

Friday December 25th
Christmas Day

Got up at 5 a.m. to have a ride on my racing bike. My father paid for it with American Express. I couldn't ride it far because of the snow, but it didn't matter. I just like looking at it. My father had written on the gift tag attached to the handlebars, 'Don't leave it out in the rain this time'—as if I would!

My parents had severe hangovers, so I took them breakfast in bed and gave them my presents at the same time. My mother was overjoyed with her egg-timer and my father was equally delighted with his bookmark, in fact everything was going OK until I casually mentioned that Bert and Queenie were my guests for the day, and would my father mind getting out of bed and picking them up in his car.

The row went on until the lousy Sugdens arrived. My Grandma and Grandad Sugden and Uncle Dennis and his wife Marcia and their son Maurice all look the same, as if they went to funerals every day of their lives. I can hardly believe that my mother is related to them. The Sugdens refused a drink and had a cup of tea whilst my mother defrosted the turkey in the bath. I helped my father carry Queenie (fifteen stone) and Bert (fourteen stone) out of our car. Queenie is one of those loud types of old ladies who dye their hair and try to look young. Bert is in love with her. He told me when I was helping him into the toilet.

Grandma Mole and Auntie Susan came at twelve-thirty and pretended to like the Sugdens. Auntie Susan told some amusing stories about life in prison but nobody but me and my father and Bert and Queenie laughed.

I went up to the bathroom and found my mother crying and running the turkey under the hot tap. She said, 'The bloody thing won't thaw out, Adrian. What am I going to do?, I said, 'Just bung it in the oven.' So she did.

We sat down to eat Christmas dinner four hours late. By then my father was too drunk to eat anything. The Sugdens enjoyed the Queen's Speech but nothing else seemed to please them. Grandma Sugden gave me a book called *Bible Stories for Boys*. I could hardly tell her that I had lost my faith, so I said thank-you and wore a false smile for so long that it hurt.

The Sugdens went to their camp beds at ten o'clock. Bert, Queenie and my mother and father played cards while I polished my bike. We all had a good time making jokes about the Sugdens. Then my father drove Bert and Queenie back to the home and I phoned Pandora up and told her that I loved her more than life itself.

I am going round to her house tomorrow to give her the deodorant and escort her to the pantomime.

Saturday December 26th
Bank Holiday in UK and Rep. of Ireland (a day may be given in lieu). **New Moon**

The Sugdens got up at 7a.m. and sat around in their best clothes looking respectable. I went out on my bike. When I got back my mother was still in bed, and my father was arguing with Grandad Sugden about our dog's behaviour, so I went for another ride.

I called in on Grandma Mole, ate four mince pies, then rode back home. I got up to 30 mph on the dual carriageway, it was dead good. I put my new suede jacket and corduroy trousers on (courtesy of my father's Barclaycard) and called for Pandora; she gave me a bottle of after-shave for my Christmas present. It was a proud moment, it signified the *End of Childhood*.

We quite enjoyed the pantomime but it was rather childish for our taste. Bill Ash and Carole Hayman were good as Aladdin and the Princess, but the robbers played by Jeff Teare and Ian Giles were best. Sue Pomeroy gave a hilarious performance as Widow Twankey. In this she was greatly helped by her cow, played by Chris Martin and Lou Wakefield.

Sunday December 27th
1st after Christmas

The Sugdens have gone back to Norfolk, thank God!

The house is back to its usual mess. My parents took a bottle of vodka and two glasses to bed with them last night. I haven't seen them since.

Went to Melton Mowbray on my bike, did it in five hours.

The Lost Boy

George Mackay Brown

There was one light in the village on Christmas Eve; it came from Jock Scabra's cottage, and he was the awkwardest old man that had ever lived in our village or in the island, or in the whole of Orkney.

I was feeling very wretched and very ill-natured myself that evening. My Aunty Belle had just been explaining to me after tea that Santa Claus, if he did exist, was a spirit that moved people's hearts to generosity and goodwill; no more or less.

Gone was my fat apple-cheeked red-coated friend of the past ten winters. Scattered were the reindeer, broken the sledge that had beaten such a marvellous path through the constellations and the Merry Dancers, while all the children of Orkney slept. Those merry perilous descents down the lum, Yule eve by Yule eve, with the sack of toys and books, games and chocolate boxes, had never really taken place at all... I looked over towards our hearth, after my aunt had finished speaking: the magic had left it, it was only a place of peat flames and peat smoke.

I can't tell you how angry I was, the more I thought about it. How deceitful, how cruel, grown-ups were! They had exiled my dear old friend, Santa Claus, to eternal oblivion. The gifts I would find in my stocking next morning would have issued from Aunty Belle's 'spirit of generosity'. It was not the same thing at all. (Most of the year I saw little enough of that spirit of generosity–at Halloween, for example, she had boxed my ears till I saw stars that had never been in the sky, for stealing a few apples and nuts out of the cupboard, before 'dooking' time.)

If there was a more ill-tempered person than my Aunty Belle in the village, it was, as I said, old Jock Scabra, the fisherman with a silver ring in his ear and a fierce one-eyed tom cat.

His house, alone in the village, was lit that night. I saw it, from our front door, at eleven o'clock.

Aunty Belle's piece of common sense had so angered me, that I was in a state of rebellion and recklessness. No, I would *not* sleep. I would not even stay in a house from which Santa had been banished. I felt utterly betrayed and bereaved.

When, about half past ten, I heard rending snores coming from Aunty Belle's bedroom, I got out of bed stealthily and put my cold clothes on, and unlatched the front door and went outside. The whole house had betrayed me—well, I intended to be out of the treacherous house when the magic hour of midnight struck.

The road through the village was deep in snow, dark except where under old Scabra's window the lamplight had stained it an orange colour. The snow shadows were blue under his walls. The stars were like sharp nails. Even though I had wrapped my scarf twice round my neck, I shivered in the bitter night.

Where could I go? The light in the old villain's window was entrancing—I fluttered towards it like a moth. How would such a sour old creature be celebrating Christmas Eve? Thinking black thoughts, beside his embers, stroking his wicked one-eyed cat.

The snow crashed like thin fragile glass under my feet.

I stood at last outside the fisherman's window. I looked in.

What I saw was astonishing beyond ghosts or trows.

There was no crotchety old man inside, no one-eyed cat, no ingrained filth and hung cobwebs. The paraffin lamp threw a circle of soft light, and all that was gathered inside that radiance was clean and pristine: the cups and plates on the dresser, the clock and ship-in-the-bottle and tea-caddies on the mantelpiece, the framed picture of Queen Victoria on the wall, the blue stones of the floor, the wood and straw of the fireside chair, the patchwork quilt on the bed.

A boy I had never seen before was sitting at the table. He might have been about my own age, and his head was a mass of bronze ringlets. On the table in front of him were an apple, an orange, a little sailing ship crudely cut from wood, with linen sails, probably cut from an old shirt. The boy—whoever he was—considered those objects with the utmost gravity. Once he put out his finger and touched the hull of the toy ship; as if it was so precious it had to be treated with special delicacy, lest it broke like a soap-bubble. I couldn't see the boy's face—only his bright hair, his lissom neck, and the gravity and joy that informed all his

157

gestures. These were his meagre Christmas presents; silently he rejoiced in them.

Beyond the circle of lamp-light, were there other dwellers in the house? There may have been hidden breath in the darkened box bed in the corner.

I don't know how long I stood in the bitter night outside. My hands were trembling. I looked down at them—they were blue with cold.

Then suddenly, for a second, the boy inside the house turned his face to the window. Perhaps he had heard the tiny splinterings of snow under my boots, or my quickened heart-beats.

The face that looked at me was Jock Scabra's, but Jock Scabra's from far back at the pure source of his life, sixty winters ago, before the ring was in his ear and before bad temper and perversity had grained black lines and furrows into his face. It was as if a cloth had been taken to a tarnished web-clogged mirror.

The boy turned back, smiling, to his Christmas hoard.

I turned and went home. I lifted the latch quietly, not to awaken Aunty Belle—for, if she knew what I had been up to that midnight, there would have been little of her 'spirit of generosity' for me. I crept, trembling, into bed.

When I woke up on Christmas morning, the 'spirit of the season' had loaded my stocking and the chair beside the bed with boxes of sweets, a Guinness Book of Records, a digital watch, a game of space wars, a cowboy hat, and a 50 pence piece. Aunty Belle stood at my bedroom door, smiling. And, 'A merry Christmas,' she said.

Breakfast over, I couldn't wait to get back to the Scabra house. The village was taken over by children with apples, snowballs, laughter as bright as bells.

I peered in at the window. All was as it had been. The piratical old man sluiced the last of his breakfast tea down his throat from a cracked saucer. He fell to picking his black-and-yellow teeth with a kipper-bone. His house was like a midden.

The one-eyed cat yawned wickedly beside the new flames in the hearth.

Christmas Morning

Frank O'Connor

I never really liked my brother, Sonny. From the time he was a baby he was always the mother's pet and always chasing her to tell her what mischief I was up to. Mind you, I was usually up to something. Until I was nine or ten I was never much good at school, and I really believe it was to spite me that he was so smart at his books. He seemed to know by instinct that this was what Mother had set her heart on, and you might almost say he spelt himself into her favour.

'Mummy,' he'd say, 'will I call Larry in to his t-e-a?' or: 'Mummy, the k-e-t-e-l is boiling,' and, of course, when he was wrong she'd correct him, and next time he'd have it right and there would be no standing him. 'Mummy,' he'd say, 'aren't I a good speller?' Cripes, we could all be good spellers if we went on like that!

Mind you, it wasn't that I was stupid. Far from it. I was just restless and not able to fix my mind for long on any one thing. I'd do the lessons for the year before, or the lessons for the year after: what I couldn't stand were the lessons we were supposed to be doing at the time. In the evenings I used to go out and play with the Doherty gang. Not, again, that I was rough, but I liked the excitement, and for the life of me I couldn't see what attracted Mother about education.

'Can't you do your lessons first and play after?' she'd say, getting white with indignation. 'You ought to be ashamed of yourself that your baby brother can read better than you.'

She didn't seem to understand that I wasn't, because there didn't seem to me to be anything particularly praiseworthy about reading, and it struck me as an occupation better suited to a sissy kid like Sonny.

'The dear knows what will become of you,' she'd say. 'If only you'd stick to your books you might be something good like a clerk or an engineer.'

'I'll be a clerk, Mummy,' Sonny would say smugly.

'Who wants to be an old clerk?' I'd say, just to annoy him. 'I'm going to be a soldier.'

'The dear knows, I'm afraid that's all you'll ever be fit for,' she would add with a sigh.

I couldn't help feeling at times that she wasn't all there. As if there was anything better a fellow could be!

Coming on to Christmas, with the days getting shorter and the shopping crowds bigger, I began to think of all the things I might get from Santa Claus. The Dohertys said there was no Santa Claus, only what your father and mother gave you, but the Dohertys were a rough class of children you wouldn't expect Santa to come to anyway. I was rooting round for whatever information I could pick up about him, but there didn't seem to be much. I was no hand with a pen, but if a letter would do any good I was ready to chance writing to him. I had plenty of initiative and was always writing off for free samples and prospectuses.

'Ah, I don't know will he come at all this year,' Mother said with a worried air. 'He has enough to do looking after steady boys who mind their lessons without bothering about the rest.'

'He only comes to good spellers, Mummy,' said Sonny. 'Isn't that right?'

'He comes to any little boy who does his best, whether he's a good speller or not,' Mother said firmly.

Well, I did my best. God knows I did! It wasn't my fault if, four days before the holiday, Flogger Dawley gave us sums we couldn't do, and Peter Doherty and myself had to go on the lang. It wasn't for love of it, for, take it from me, December is no month for mitching, and we spent most of our time sheltering from the rain in a store on the quays. The only mistake we made was imagining we could keep it up till the holidays without being spotted. That showed real lack of foresight.

Of course, Flogger Dawley noticed and sent home word to know what was keeping me. When I came in on the third day the mother gave me a look I'll never forget, and said: 'Your dinner is there.' She was too full to talk. When I tried to explain to her about Flogger Dawley and the sums she brushed it aside and said: 'You have no word.' I saw then it wasn't the langing she minded but the lies, though I still didn't see how you could lang without lying. She didn't speak to me for days. And even then I couldn't

161

make out what she saw in education, or why she wouldn't let me grow up naturally like anyone else.

To make things worse, it stuffed Sonny up more than ever. He had the air of one saying: 'I don't know what they'd do without me in this blooming house.' He stood at the front door, leaning against the jamb with his hands in his trouser pockets, trying to make himself look like Father, and shouted to the other kids so that he could be heard all over the road.

'Larry isn't left go out. He went on the lang with Peter Doherty and me mother isn't talking to him.'

And at night, when we were in bed, he kept it up.

'Santa Claus won't bring you anything this year, aha!'

'Of course he will,' I said.

'How do you know?'

'Why wouldn't he?'

'Because you went on the lang with Doherty. I wouldn't play with them Doherty fellows.'

'You wouldn't be left.'

'I wouldn't play with them. They're no class. They had the bobbies up to the house.'

'And how would Santa know I was on the lang with Peter Doherty?' I growled, losing patience with the little prig.

'Of course he'd know. Mummy would tell him.'

'And how could Mummy tell him and he up at the North Pole? Poor Ireland, she's rearing them yet! 'Tis easy seen you're only an old baby.'

'I'm not a baby, and I can spell better than you, and Santa won't bring you anything.'

'We'll see whether he will or not,' I said sarcastically, doing the old man on him.

But, to tell the God's truth, the old man was only bluff. You could never tell what powers these superhuman chaps would have of knowing what you were up to. And I had a bad conscience about the langing because I'd never before seen the mother like that.

That was the night I decided that the only sensible thing to do was to see Santa myself and explain to him. Being a man, he'd probably understand. In those days I was a good-looking kid and had a way with me when I liked. I had only to smile nicely at one old gent on the North Mall to get a penny from him, and I felt if only I could get Santa by himself I could do the same with him and maybe get something worth while from him. I wanted a model railway: I was sick of Ludo and Snakes-and-Ladders.

I started to practise lying awake, counting five hundred and then a thousand, and trying to hear first eleven, then midnight, from Shandon. I felt sure Santa would be round by midnight, seeing that he'd be coming from the north, and would have the whole of the South Side to do afterwards. In some ways I was very farsighted. The only trouble was the things I was farsighted about.

I was so wrapped up in my own calculations that I had little attention to spare for Mother's difficulties. Sonny and I used to go to town with her, and while she was shopping we stood outside a toyshop in the North Main Street, arguing about what we'd like for Christmas.

On Christmas Eve when Father came home from work and gave her the housekeeping money, she stood looking at it doubtfully while her face grew white.

'Well?' he snapped, getting angry. 'What's wrong with that?'

'What's wrong with it?' she muttered. 'On Christmas Eve!'

'Well,' he asked truculently, sticking his hands in his trouser pockets as though to guard what was left, 'do you think I get more because it's Christmas?'

163

'Lord God,' she muttered distractedly. 'And not a bit of cake in the house, nor a candle, nor anything!'

'All right,' he shouted, beginning to stamp. 'How much will the candle be?'

'Ah, for pity's sake,' she cried, 'will you give me the money and not argue like that before the children? Do you think I'll leave them with nothing on the one day of the year?'

'Bad luck to you and your children!' he snarled. 'Am I to be slaving from one year's end to another for you to be throwing it away on toys? Here,' he added, tossing two half-crowns on the table, 'that's all you're going to get, so make the most of it.'

'I suppose the publicans will get the rest,' she said bitterly.

Later she went into town, but did not bring us with her, and returned with a lot of parcels, including the Christmas candle. We waited for Father to come home to his tea, but he didn't, so we had our own tea and a slice of Christmas cake each, and then Mother put Sonny on a chair with the holy-water stoup to sprinkle the candle, and when he lit it she said: 'The light of heaven to our souls.' I could see she was upset because Father wasn't in—it should be the oldest and youngest. When we hung up our stockings at bedtime he was still out.

Then began the hardest couple of hours I ever put in. I was mad with sleep but afraid of losing the model railway, so I lay for a while, making up things to say to Santa when he came. They varied in tone from frivolous to grave, for some old gents like kids to be modest and well-spoken, while others prefer them with spirit. When I had rehearsed them all I tried to wake Sonny to keep me company, but that kid slept like the dead.

Eleven struck from Shandon, and soon after I heard the latch, but it was only Father coming home.

'Hello, little girl,' he said, letting on to be surprised at finding Mother waiting up for him, and then broke into a self-conscious giggle. 'What have you up so late?'

'Do you want your supper?' she asked shortly.

'Ah, no, no,' he replied. 'I had a bit of pig's cheek at Daneen's on my way up (Daneen was my uncle). I'm very fond of a bit of pig's cheek.... My goodness, is it that late?' he exclaimed, letting on to be astonished. 'If I knew that I'd have gone to the North Chapel for midnight Mass. I'd like to hear the *Adeste* again. That's a hymn I'm very fond of—a most touching hymn.'

165

Then he began to hum it falsetto.

Adeste fideles
Solus domus dagus.

Father was very fond of Latin hymns, particularly when he had
a drop in, but as he had no notion of the words he made them up
as he went along, and this always drove Mother mad.

'Ah, you disgust me!' she said in a scalded voice, and closed the
room door behind her. Father laughed as if he thought it a great
joke; and he struck a match to light his pipe and for a while puffed
at it noisily. The light under the door dimmed and went out but he
continued to sing emotionally.

Dixie medearo
Tutum tonum tantum
Venite adoremus.

He had it all wrong but the effect was the same on me. To save
my life I couldn't keep awake.

Coming on to dawn, I woke with the feeling that something
dreadful had happened. The whole house was quiet, and the little
bedroom that looked out on the foot and a half of back yard was
pitch-dark. It was only when I glanced at the window that I saw
how all the silver had drained out of the sky. I jumped out of bed
to feel my stocking, well knowing that the worst had happened.
Santa had come while I was asleep, and gone away with an
entirely false impression of me, because all he had left me was
some sort of book, folded up, a pen and pencil, and a tuppenny
bag of sweets. Not even Snakes-and-Ladders! For a while I was
too stunned even to think. A fellow who was able to drive over
rooftops and climb down chimneys without getting stuck—God,
wouldn't you think he'd know better?

Then I began to wonder what that foxy boy, Sonny, had. I
went to his side of the bed and felt his stocking. For all his spelling
and sucking-up he hadn't done so much better, because, apart
from a bag of sweets like mine, all Santa had left him was a popgun, one that fired a cork on a piece of string and which you could
get in any huxter's shop for sixpence.

All the same, the fact remained that it was a gun, and a gun was
better than a book any day of the week. The Dohertys had a gang,
and the gang fought the Strawberry Lane kids who tried to play

football on our road. That gun would be very useful to me in many ways, while it would be lost on Sonny who wouldn't be let play with the gang, even if he wanted to.

Then I got the inspiration, as it seemed to me, direct from heaven. Suppose I took the gun and gave Sonny the book! Sonny would never be any good in the gang: he was fond of spelling, and a studious child like him could learn a lot of spellings from a book like mine. As he hadn't seen Santa any more than I had, what he hadn't seen wouldn't grieve him. I was doing no harm to anyone; in fact, if Sonny only knew, I was doing him a good turn which he might have cause to thank me for later. That was one thing I was always keen on; doing good turns. Perhaps this was Santa's intention the whole time and he had merely become confused between us. It was a mistake that might happen to anyone. So I put the book, the pencil, and the pen into Sonny's stocking and the popgun into my own, and returned to bed and slept again. As I say, in those days I had plenty of initiative.

It was Sonny who woke me, shaking me to tell me that Santa had come and left me a gun. I let on to be surprised and rather disappointed in the gun, and to divert his mind from it made him show me his picture book, and cracked it up to the skies.

As I knew, that kid was prepared to believe anything, and

nothing would do him then but to take the presents in to show Father and Mother. This was a bad moment for me. After the way she had behaved about the langing, I distrusted Mother, though I had the consolation of believing that the only person who could contradict me was now somewhere up by the North Pole. That gave me a certain confidence, so Sonny and I burst in with our presents, shouting: 'Look what Santa Claus brought!'

Father and Mother woke, and Mother smiled, but only for an instant. As she looked at me her face changed. I knew that look; I knew it only too well. It was the same she had worn the day I came home from langing, when she said I had no word.

'Larry,' she said in a low voice, 'where did you get that gun?'

'Santa left it in my stocking, Mummy,' I said, trying to put on an injured air, though it baffled me how she guessed that he hadn't. 'He did, honest.'

'You stole it from that poor child's stocking while he was asleep,' she said, her voice quivering with indignation. 'Larry, Larry, how could you be so mean?'

'Now, now, now,' Father said deprecatingly, ''tis Christmas morning.'

'Ah,' she said with real passion, 'it's easy it comes to you. Do you think I want my son to grow up a liar and a thief?'

'Ah, what thief, woman?' he said testily. 'Have sense, can't you?' He was as cross if you interrupted him in his benevolent moods as if they were of the other sort, and this one was probably exacerbated by a feeling of guilt for his behaviour of the night before. 'Here, Larry,' he said, reaching out for the money on the bedside table, 'here's sixpence for you and one for Sonny. Mind you don't lose it now!'

But I looked at Mother and saw what was in her eyes. I burst out crying, threw the popgun on the floor, and ran bawling out of the house before anyone on the road was awake. I rushed up the lane behind the house and threw myself on the wet grass.

I understood it all, and it was almost more than I could bear: that there was no Santa Claus, as the Dohertys said, only Mother trying to scrape together a few coppers from the housekeeping; that Father was mean and common and a drunkard, and that she had been relying on me to raise her out of the misery of the life she was leading. And I knew that the look in her eyes was the fear that, like my father, I should turn out to be mean and common and a drunkard.

An Assault on Santa Claus

Timothy Callender

When Barry first heard of Santa Claus, he was puzzled. He wanted to make sure that his grandfather had heard aright.

'You mean, you never know?' his grandfather asked. 'Santa Claus never bring nothing for you at Christmas yet?'

'No,' Barry said.

'Lord, boy, I could imagine how you does behave when you inside you parents home,' Grandfather said. 'Is only when you behave good that you can get any presents from Santa Claus.'

Barry nodded slowly.

'You must try and behave good this Christmas,' Grandfather said. 'I feel sure that if you behave good he may leave something for you when he pass through.'

'Is a whole lot of children he have to visit. You think he have enough toys for all of them?'

'Yes, man. Santa Claus always carry along the exact amount of toys.'

Barry thought about it all the Christmas season. He couldn't understand how Santa Claus would find out, but he made sure that he behaved himself. He was very obedient to all his grandfather said. Day by day he restrained himself from numerous temptations. He hoped that Santa was taking careful note of it all.

'You sure he know how good I behaving?' he asked his grandfather.

'Santa know what you deserve,' Grandfather said. 'You just wait and see if he don't bring the same carpentry set that you say you would like for Christmas.'

So Barry hoped, with the same fervour that he hoped Santa was noticing his good behaviour. All things considered, it was an easy way to gain a valuable gift.

It was a remarkable change. Grandfather was pleased. 'Why you can't behave so all the while?' he asked. 'Is the first time I ever see

169

you so quiet and obedient. I hear all about how you was behaving before, you know. Your parents tell me how much trouble you always getting youself into. They tell me how you always fighting at school, how you always getting licks, and how you involve yuhself with the police and Probation Officer too. But look how nice you behaving now. Why you can't behave so all the while?'

'Is all them boys that does interfere with me first,' Barry muttered.

'I must tell yuh parents how well you behave all the time you spend vacation here with me.'

Barry nodded.

Christmas Eve came. Barry was in a state of suppressed excitement all day. Evening took long in coming.

'Tonight is the night,' Grandfather said at supper. 'You mustn't forget to put out something for Santa to drop presents in.'

'Is all right,' Barry said. 'I have a crocus bag tie onto the bedstead.'

Grandfather laughed. 'No boy. You can't make it look like you expect everything. A crocus bag look too greedy. Why you don't put a ordinary paper bag?'

'All right,' Barry said. But he didn't like it much. He had begun to feel that he had behaved well long enough to deserve more than a paper bag of gifts, even if the carpentry set was one of them. Santa had a whole big bag of gifts, and plenty more where they came from. He wondered how he could outwit Santa as he hung up his paper bag. Wondered if it was possible for Santa to make a mistake and give him more than he intended.

'We'll have to leave the window open,' he told Grandfather. 'We ain't have no chimney on this house.'

'Is all right,' Grandfather answered, and laughed. 'Is obvious to me that you never hear 'bout the things Santa can do. You ain't know he could even come through the keyhole?'

'He come just like a magic-man, then,' Barry said.

'You kin say so. But remember, he ain't going come unless you fall asleep, because he really don't like no children to see him.'

'All right, I going to bed now,' Barry said.

Grandfather smiled when he left. He know that Barry, like every other one of his grandsons, would stay awake to see Santa Claus.

Barry lay down without sleeping. His eyes were open but he

was very still. He could hear his heartbeat sounding through the pillow. He heard the clock strike midnight. Santa must come sometime soon.

He had barely begun to doze when the sound of the door lock woke him. He stiffened. From where he lay he looked directly past his feet toward the door. The door was swinging open. Barry's heart raced.

He saw the figure in the doorway; big, fat, covered in red silky clothes. The light from the street outside came through the window silhouetting him. Barry saw the huge grey bag on his shoulder, heard the clinks and knocks of many things inside the bag. Barry's heart raced. He knew he was going to attempt something no child had attempted before. He wanted the whole bag of toys.

As Santa stepped forward and bent over the paper bag at the foot of the bed, Barry reached over the side of the bed, down to the floor. He gripped his grandfather's mighty walking stick and brought it up with a grunt. He barely made out Santa's head, and he aimed and let fly. Whang! The bag flew from Santa's shoulder. Santa clapped his hands to his head and tumbled on the floor.

Barry sprang from the bed. He was halfway out of the room with Santa's bag on his shoulder when he heard his grandfather's voice: 'Lord have mercy, uh dead, uh dead!'

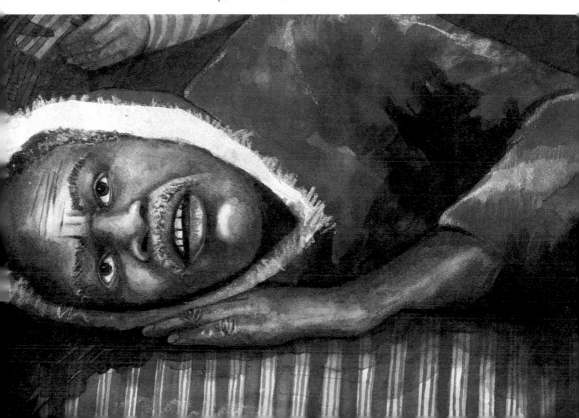

The Anarchist's Pudding

Geraldine McCaughrean

He lived in the attic, and came and went by an outside staircase, so that he did not have to pass through the house. The walls of the stairs and hall were painted a particularly cheerful red, and it would never do for an anarchist like Katskinner to waver in his discontent. He had long since stopped using the living room with its comfortable inglenook fireplace and chintz chairs, and the bedroom too, with its pretty view of the castle. He had ripped out the doorbell, sealed up the letterbox (so that his copy of *Anarchist's Monthly* was not delivered there by mistake) and installed a two-ring cooker in the attic. There he huddled, in a holey track-suit, and pondered how to wreak his terrible revenge on the King.

Katskinner had good reason to hate King Goodfellow. Ever since the Coronation, his reign had been one long round of reform. First there was the 'Outings for Everyone' Act, then the Abolition of Taxes, closely followed by the *Gripe and Grievance Bill* which installed royal suggestion boxes on all street corners. Little by little, one by one, every complaint, every injustice, every source of discontent had been expunged from life in Superbia.

People said he was kind. People said no trouble was too great for him. People said that life had never been so enjoyable in all the history of Superbia. But Katskinner knew what Goodfellow was about. All this kindness—it was a subversive and covert attack on Anarchy. Goodfellow was hell-bent on exterminating discontent and putting Anarchists permanently out of work.

Goodfellow was a formidable enemy: he had almost achieved his appalling goal. Katskinner was now the only, yes the sole, lonely Anarchist in the whole of Superbia.

He had tried to stir up fury among the teachers, telling them that all chance would soon be gone of civil war, revolts, assassinations and coups—all those exciting things that go to fill history books. But they said they could get by teaching all the

172

history up to the Coronation of Goodfellow, when there had been plenty of wars. Katskinner had tried to make Anarchists out of the gun manufacturers, arguing that Goodfellow had put them out of work. But they were too busy manufacturing flags for the Big Parades and tinsel for Christmas. They said they preferred doing that to making guns.

Christmas! Katskinner's worst time of year was just round the corner. At Christmas the most sour and surly people—the most promising Anarchists—became friendly and smiling and peaceable. When he knocked on doors to sow the seeds of discontent, people only gave him a glass of sherry and showed him the scarves they were knitting for distant relations. This year Katskinner was determined: Christmas and King Goodfellow had to go.

He told the milkman: 'Look at all the extra work it makes— cream! turkeys! Tell your colleagues—protest! Revolt!' But the milkman only thrust a bottle of milk into his hand and said it was the only day of the year milkmen got as holiday and that he would kick Katskinner down his outside stairs before he let him abolish Christmas.

Katskinner went to the shopkeeper and said, 'Look at all the trade you lose, closing for two whole days!'

But the shopkeeper only rang up 'No Sale' on the till and gave Katskinner a pound. 'I sell so much before Christmas that it takes me two days to count the extra money. Now you go along and buy yourself a seasonal drink on me. You look fair pinched with cold.'

Katskinner appealed to the postman. 'All those Christmas cards! The holly wreaths over the letter boxes! Protest! Revolt! Sabotage! They couldn't have Christmas without you!'

'I'll think about it,' said the postman doubtfully and gave Katskinner a wad of cards and letters. The Anarchist crammed them into his coat pocket and thundered, exasperated, down the outside stairs.

After the postman he tried the clergymen, the travel agents, the doctor. But they only told him they were sorry he was unhappy: the doctor gave him some pills to help him sleep. Then they got on with preparing for Christmas.

Last of all, Katskinner tried the baker. 'All those Christmas cakes! And puddings! Revolt! Protest!'

'I like making puddings,' said the baker. 'I make the best

puddings in the whole country!' And he held one up. It raised Katskinner's hopes for a moment: the baker looked just like an Anarchist with the pudding balanced on the palm of his hand like a big round bomb.

'That's it!' cried Katskinner. 'A pudding!' And he rushed home, his eyes gleaming brighter than any Machiavelli.

He took cordite and currants, gelignite and gelatine, cartridges and caster sugar, micro-circuitry and marzipan, gunpowder and baking powder, fuller's earth and flour. He mixed them all together in a bowl, following the recipe he found in *Anarchist's Monthly*. And wrapping the mixture in a large pudding cloth, he boiled it up on his two-ring stove. When it was done, he concealed a time-lapse detonator under a sprig of holly, sprinkled it with icing sugar and ethyl alcohol, and put it in a big cardboard box.

'With Goodfellow out of the way, there'll be a struggle for power—lots of people nobody likes trying to grab the crown—lots of foreign princes and American advisers arriving by every train. Not long before I'll have would-be Anarchists queuing up at my door. They'll be begging me to accept the title of Generalissimo Guerrilla—Generalissimo Katskinner. I'll change the history of Superbia!'

In rummaging for a scrap of paper to label and address his parcel, he took the letters out of his pocket. 'Christmas cards, huh!' he snarled, flinging them to right and left in disgust. The doorbell rang. It was the postman again.

'Compliments of the season, sir. Can I have a word?'

'No time. I'm busy. Here, take this.' (He wrote on the box itself.) 'Here's a pound for the postage. Can't stop to bandy words with a reactionary lackey. Bye!' And he slammed the door in the postman's face.

Only one envelope remained in his hand. He was just about to throw it aside when he saw the crest in one corner: the royal crest. It was a letter from the King.

Katskinner's hands trembled a little as he read it. It gave him a most peculiar feeling to see his own name in the King's splendid copperplate handwriting.

> *My dear Katskinner,*
> *As you may know, it has been my aim, as King, to strive for universal harmony and happiness among the peoples of Superbia.*

But in this it seems I have failed.

It has come to my attention that you are not contented, my dear Katskinner—that in trying to make others content I have left no outlet for your ambitions and very real talents. This deeply distresses me, particularly at this time of year, when everybody should be basking in well-being. I wonder if you would come and discuss the matter with me over Christmas lunch? It preys on my mind, and I think I might have a solution! Compliments of the season.

Your affectionate despot,
Goodfellow (R)

The hairs rose on the nape of Katskinner's neck. He screwed up the letter, then he flattened it out again against his thigh with the palm of his hand. 'Why not?' he murmured. 'Dangerous—but then we Anarchists have to accept an element of risk... And it's the perfect alibi! I'll stay for the first course, then find some excuse to leave before the pudding's served... Exquisite. Quite exquisite...' And he spent some time standing in front of the mirror, practising his cruel-satanic look, and fluffing out his eyebrows until he looked sufficiently menacing.

At the palace next day—Christmas Day—he was received with elaborate good manners. A footman took his black leather coat. Another brought him a glass of sherry on a silver tray. The Royal Superbia Symphonia were ranged up and down the grand staircase, playing a selection of carols, while choir boys in red surplices and big white ruffs carolled along the landing.

'Forced to work on a public holiday?' said Katskinner to the Royal Superbia Symphonia. 'Protest! Revolt! Refuse!' And to the choir boys he said, 'Child labour! Exploitation of minors! Protest, boys! Revolt!' But they only offered him snowy marshmallows, and went on singing.

'Ah, Katskinner! Happy Christmas!' The King stood, arms spread wide, in the doorway of the banqueting hall. 'So glad you could come! What a nice jumper! Was it a Christmas Present? This was—don't say anything, the Queen crocheted it. Warm enough? Come in by the fire. I turn the central heating off at Christmas: the servants insist it's not the same without log fires to light on Christmas morning. There's just a few other people: hope you don't mind. But *you* must sit next to me. I have to discuss *Plans* with you!'

'Can't stop long,' said Katskinner. 'Have to write a paper on the Dissolution of the Monarchy by teatime.' But he let Goodfellow draw him by the elbow into the great dining hall.

The wood-smokey warmth and array of smells made him quite faint for a moment: duck and oranges, watercress soup, fresh bread, brandy sauce, hot chocolate, roast potatoes, broccoli and stuffing, horsechestnuts and clementines, figs and coffee... You can't cook much but baked beans and soup on a two-ring burner.

The wine was purple and French. Katskinner took one sip and decided to nationalize it, after the Revolution. He drank three glasses before the soup came round.

The Chancellor, who was sitting six chairs down, made a speech about Peace, Prosperity and the tie the Queen had so kindly crocheted for him. The Archbishop, seated forty-four chairs down, gave thanks for the dinner and the similar handkerchief he had received. The King asked Katskinner if he would like to make a toast. So Katskinner got up and raised his glass. 'Down with Christmas and King Goodfellow!'

Everyone thought it was hilarious. 'Good old Katskinner! Same as ever! Ho, ho, ho!' they said, and raised their glasses. 'Up with Christmas and King Goodfellow and Katskinner!' Katskinner had another glass of wine.

When he looked at his watch, the hands seemed to be inside out or upside down. He had to ask the King what time it was.

'Time for the duck!' declared the King, and the duck—or rather one hundred and twenty ducks came in—on golden salvers, blooming with orange peel and sprigs of basil.

The duck tasted of childhood—childhood Christmas days in Muscovy, with basted, golden duck and honeyed milk, and feather races on the river and low, warm houses with red walls and carpets, and the view beyond the banks of the Covy, and fireworks in a black velvet sky...

No, it didn't taste of fireworks. It was the *King* who was talking about fireworks, sowing mischievous memories in Katskinner's heart.

'It's time I was going,' he said, finishing up his wine.

'But you can't go yet! I haven't finished telling you about my Plan!' said Goodfellow, refilling Katskinner's glass. 'These fireworks for the New Year celebrations—they wouldn't be the only ones. There'd be fireworks at Easter and fireworks to

177

celebrate turning back the clocks, and Midsummer fireworks, and next year even Christmas fireworks... that's all supposing you want the job.'

'Job? What job?'

'The job of Master of Fireworks, of course! That's what I've been telling you. I'm offering you unlimited funds and all the old stocks of gunpowder (now that the munitions factories have gone over to making tinsel and flags). I thought it might appeal to you. I'll throw in Minister of Demolition if you're undecided.'

Katskinner peered into the King's face. 'No limit on bangs?'

'As loud as you like.'

'Or flashes?'

'Just so long as nobody gets hurt.'

'Or colours?'

'The more the merrier. I like those ones that go whoop-whoop-*whoop*! and spiral off in all directions,' said Goodfellow.

'Oh so do I! And those rockets that explode again just when you think they've finished...'

'And Roman candles, of course...'

'And the big end-pieces—you know, a hammer and sickle all done in red Vesuviuses—and those great big mortars that spill stars all over the...' In flinging his arms wide, Katskinner almost knocked the Christmas pudding out of the hands of the butler standing behind him. He gave a kind of strangled gulp then, looking down the room, saw that a hundred and twenty Christmas puddings, all looking exactly like his bomb, had entered, in stainless steel bowls. There was an overpowering smell of alcohol.

Katskinner put two hands to his chair and leapt up to run. But suddenly, inexplicably, like some terrible joke played at his expense, the lights went out. One candle, far down the table, dimly illuminated a few of the hovering puddings.

'Right!' said King Goodfellow gleefully. 'Light the brandy and let the puddings burn!'

'Oh my....' Katskinner fell out of his chair. It was too dark to see the door: he could not remember where it stood. His legs seemed to be purple and French and made totally of liquid. He put both arms over his head and waited for the explosion. Each butler solemnly struck a match and held it to his pudding.

'Aaaah!' There was a sentimental sigh of delight from a hundred

places round the table. Katskinner opened his eyes and found himself peering over the edge of the table. A long column of a hundred and twenty glowing puddings, like orderly planets spinning in their vaporous auras of purple flame, lit the happy faces of the guests. Katskinner looked at his watch. His bomb had been due to explode ten minutes before.

'Katskinner, I do believe you've had a drop more wine than is good for you,' said the King, leaning over the arm of his chair to pat Katskinner on the head.

'Yes, your Majesty.'

'Well, about that job: have some pudding, and think about it. You don't have to decide now. Let me know in the morning.'

'No pudding. No. Thank you, your Majesty.'

'No pudding? But that's the best bit! There's cream *and* brandy sauce—and sixteen silver joeys in every pudding. I commissioned them specially from the baker in town. He's reputed to make the best puddings in the country, you know.'

'All of them? You mean you didn't get...' Katskinner let the question tail away, and the silence was filled by the merry ringing of bells as a fire engine rushed by beneath the windows.

As Katskinner left, the Royal Superbia Symphonia had just finished their dinner, too, and were slouched about, up and down the stairs, with their cummerbunds undone and their faces fiery red above their unfastened collars. They struck up a discordant but well-meant verse of '*Ding Dong Merrily on High.*'

The fire service reached Katskinner's house long before he did. By the time he arrived, they had the fire under control. Only the attic and roof were missing. The explosion had lifted them off like a gent lifting his hat to a lady. The rest of the house was perfectly untouched, although the hose-water made rather a mess of the red wallpaper and stair-carpet.

A considerable crowd had gathered to watch the fire: their faces were lit with an orange glow that made them look festive in the early dark of late afternoon. The face next to Katskinner turned to him and said, 'Could I have a word, do you think?' It was the postman.

'It's not the time... The top just got blown off my house,' said Katskinner peevishly.

'Yes, I know. And I think I did it, you see. Awfully sorry. But it was that parcel, wasn't it?'

180

'What parcel?'

'That parcel you gave me to post yesterday. Well, I thought about what you said, you see—about the holly wreaths over the letter boxes and all those Christmas cards. And I.. well, I decided I *would* revolt, after all. I decided to be an Anarchist like you and refuse to deliver any more letters or parcels. Only unfortunately yours was the only one left. Everyone else had posted all their cards and presents by Christmas Eve. So I put yours back at the top of the outside staircase. This morning. I rang the bell to tell you, but you'd gone out. I don't know, Mr Katskinner. I'm not awfully sure about this Anarchy business. It seems to make a lot of trouble for nice people like the Fire Brigade... And you, Mr Katskinner. I'm glad you were out.'

Katskinner scratched his beard and found in it a few crumbs of the baker's excellent Christmas pudding. He ate them as he considered his response to the postman.

'Yes, I was out,' he said. 'I was up at the palace, actually. Invited to Christmas dinner by the King.'

'*Really*? How fantastically marvellous for you!'

'Well, it was a matter of business, really,' said Katskinner with extreme nonchalance. 'He wanted to offer me the job of Master of Fireworks.'

'Amazing! Wonderful! And did you accept?'

'We-e-e-ll,' said Katskinner very very slowly. 'I got him to throw in Minister of Demolitions before I said yes. By the way, I don't think I extended to you the compliments of the season, did I? Happy Christmas. Yes indeed. You'll deliver the post to the *front* door in future, won't you?'

And stepping over a coil of hosepipe, Katskinner let himself in to the ground floor of his pleasant little house, and made himself tea and toast, using the big gas-stove in the kitchen. He ate it in front of a blazing fire in the living-room grate, while enjoying the view of the castle where a light was burning in every window.

Christmas in the Floods

Olaf Ruhen

It was just four days to go to Christmas when the flood began, and I guess you wouldn't believe what a heartbreak it is to have a flood at Christmas time; especially a Christmas when everybody was working so hard to make it good. We wanted to make this Christmas something special, because of the way Dad was feeling about Tommy.

Just after lunch I saddled up old Stone and rode right up to the tops of the hills, looking out to find where the best Christmas bush was growing, and I gathered a big armful, real bright-red stuff, on long branches. Mum always said you couldn't have an Australian Christmas without Christmas bush; but she didn't know what was coming up for us that year.

I rode home the long way, by the swamp, and the Christmas bells were like a carpet; red and gold lilies so bright and thick they were like an acre of flames. And last of all, just a little way from home, I went aside to follow along the banks of the creek, because I wanted to mark a she-oak good enough to serve for a Christmas tree. There aren't any pines in our part of the country; but the she-oaks look like the real thing when they're young.

I was away all the afternoon, and just as I came to the garden fence near the house the rain came down; great big splashes of rain that spread as big as saucers.

Ralph was at the trough with the team. He started to ask me how far I'd had to go for the Christmas bush. He liked to get up in the hills himself, but since Tommy had left he hadn't that much time. But Dad saw him from the door of the smithy where he was working.

'You hurry up and get the team fed,' Dad said. 'And Dave, get the cow in. Then you can turn Stone out in the back paddock against the Hundred-Acre.'

'Aw, gee, Dad,' I said, but he had gone back to the forge.

'The river's going to rise,' Ralph told me. 'The radio's carried flood warnings all afternoon, Gran says.'

We didn't say anything about Dad getting on our backs like that. He had been a bit touchy and hard to get on with ever since Tommy left home. It began when Tommy came home from school and announced that he wasn't going to have anything to do with the farm. He wanted to study for the Air Force and be a pilot; and he had to get Dad's permission because he was only seventeen. There was a big row, and Tommy left. He got a job with a radio store, but Dad was hurt because he had been counting on Tommy. He took it all out on Ralph. Ralph was a bit slow. He could do anything at all with the stock, but he just didn't have any notion when it came to business; while Tommy was as sharp as a tack. I guess Dad thought I was too young to take much account of. I was only thirteen then, last August. Ralph and I had the same birthday, only he was seven years older.

I got soaked to the skin getting Daisy into the byre; and while I was milking her the rain was making big splashes like little teapots in the pools in the yard, although it had been dry only half an hour before. Then I had to take Stone down to the back paddock. There wasn't much shelter there, up on the rise, but the lower paddocks near the river weren't safe in a flood.

All night the radio was giving flood warnings; and before I went to bed the last warning said that the peak of the flood would reach Singleton next day at noon.

'That's four in the afternoon for us,' said Dad. 'Good job it'll be daylight.'

We were sitting on the wide verandah, and I was helping Mum paint a little cut-down barrel for a tub for the Christmas tree. We couldn't see out into the night at all. It was just driving storm, and the lights were catching the raindrops. They looked like silver lances.

'Do you think it'll catch the house?' asked Mum, and Dad said, 'Could do.'

'Your father built this house,' said Gran. 'He built it strong and true, and he had an eye for every risk. This house will be safe from floods. Your father thought of everything. That's why he would never rest till he bought the Hundred-Acre at the top of the rise.'

Our place faces the river, and there are four hundred acres of flat, rich bottom-land. From there on the land slopes up and we had six hundred acres under sheep. The house is near the foot of these slopes, half a mile and more back from the river; and behind the house is the end of a long gravelly ridge, running right back towards the hills, and cut through with three or four little gullies which feed the creek on the other side. That's our Hundred-Acre.

'I've got a beaut tree picked out,' I told Mum.

'I'll bet you have,' she said and she laughed.

I was just going to bed when a flash announcement came through on the radio, with another flood warning.

'At 8.25 tonight flood-waters in a crest twenty feet high burst levees at Georgetown. Casualties are feared. Further details will be announced as they come in.'

Mother looked up anxiously. 'It's a bad one,' she said.

'First thing in the morning we'll shift all the stock up the Hundred-Acre, Ralph,' Dad said.

I said good-night to them all then and went to bed.

We'd had a flood in the house before. It came half-way up the table-legs. We had shifted all the carpets and the rugs into the attic rooms, and all the furniture that mattered. The water stayed in the house a day and a half. But if it didn't worry Dad, it didn't worry me and I went to sleep soon.

When I woke next morning the rain was coming down harder than ever. The river had risen, and it covered the bottom paddock. Dad and Ralph were down there, working with a mob of sheep caught on a little rise.

The sheep had panicked, and they wouldn't swim to the other side of the water, and Dad and Ralph were wading waist-deep, catching the sheep and bringing them one at a time back to the dry land near the house. Rab and Spot, our two herding dogs, were helping them. I dressed as quick as I could and went down to help. Mum sent a basket of food with me, because they had had no breakfast.

The water was creeping up all the time, thick brown water, and the little grass frogs were swimming in it. And the whole surface of the water was covered with spiders and beetles and every kind of insect you could think of. I had my feet bare, and I kept a look-out for the spiders, because there are poisonous kinds here that are quite deadly.

'I'll give you a hand,' I offered.

'It's a bit deep for you,' Ralph said. So I said I'd get the cow in and milk her after breakfast. When they started to eat we were standing on dry ground, and when they had finished the water was up to my ankles.

Well, we worked all morning. It rained and rained and we were soaked all the time, but it was warm and we didn't mind. After lunch I thought of something: if I wanted that Christmas tree I'd better hurry. So I took a tomahawk and went out to get it. And when I found the tree, it was standing in a foot of water.

I was away about three hours, I suppose, because I was on foot, and the tree got a bit heavy, even if it was only about seven feet tall. But I thought they'd be pleased that we had a tree for Christmas after all. But Dad roared at me.

'Where the devil have you been?' he shouted. 'You stay close to the house. And what the dickens do you think you're going to do with that damn-fool rubbish?'

I felt sore about that. If I'd been a kid I'd have felt like crying, because I thought he'd like me to have remembered the Christmas tree. But it made Mum happy.

'Your father's worried, Dave,' she said. 'He doesn't really mean it.' Then she looked at the tree. 'Oh, it's a lovely tree!'

I got the tub and wedged the tree in it tightly with bricks and stones, and covered them over with earth.

I was still looking at the tree when Dad came running into the house and called for me to give him a hand, and we started shifting things into the attic room. Mum and even Gran came running too. But we had only rolled up the carpet off one floor when the water came up into the house. Dad said he had seen it coming down the valley like a wall. He and Ralph had shifted all the stock into the Hundred-Acre by that time; everything outside was safe, and now Ralph had gone off somewhere.

We worked like mad, and we got the attic rooms crammed with some of the smaller furniture. We were still working when it was coming dark. I had a Christmas present for Mum and one for Dad, and I hadn't bought the others yet. But I sneaked those two up the stairs without anyone seeing me, and I hid them under my shirts in the drawer.

Just before dark Ralph came down the hill. He waded right up to his neck in water, and then he had to swim a hundred yards.

When he came to where the garden had been he walked again, but the water was up to his armpits, and the current was running strong just as it does in the middle of the river.

Dad waited till he got in and climbed the stairs, and then he bawled him out too. 'Hell of a time to go off on your own,' he said. Dad didn't usually swear like that. He was hurt and sore and worried.

'Nicholson's stock were up against the fence,' Ralph said. 'I cut the wires and let them into our Hundred-Acre. Then I went round and Peters was having trouble. I cut the wires there too; and then I gave him a hand for a while. He's lost stock. Lost a lot of it.'

'Hasn't Peters got high ground of his own?' Dad asked. He didn't really want Ralph to tell him. He was mad clear through. 'There's not more than a scratching of feed for our own stock on the Hundred-Acre. What the dickens do you think we're going to feed them on?'

'They're neighbours,' Ralph said.

I didn't like Dad talking like that. I went out and down the stairs again. It was up near my shoulders on the ground floor, and it was dark and the water seemed cold now, and there were wriggly things in it. I felt my way out on the veranda, and the tree was there in its tub. I grabbed it by the branches and tried to pull it, and it came easily in the water, so I worked it round through the doors and back to the stairs. I got it up the first four stairs all right, but then the tub was half out of the water, and it got mighty heavy.

I was pulling at it and I fell, and the tree fell with me. I must have made some sort of noise, because Dad came down.

'For heaven's sake, we don't want that kind of rubbish up there,' he said. 'We haven't got room to move as it is. Haven't any of you boys got any sense at all?'

Twice, once early in the night, and once after midnight, it stopped raining and there was a break in the cloud. We had no electricity now, and had to use storm lanterns, and we couldn't hear anything on the radio; the water came higher and higher on the stairs. Outside, when the moon came out, the current raced on both sides of us.

Further out in the current there was stock going down the river. The beasts were all swimming, cattle and pigs mostly, only a few sheep, but they were all swimming with the current, and we didn't think there was much hope for them.

I went to sleep, but Ralph wakened me. It was still dark, but there was a little light coming, and I knew there was only one more day to Christmas Eve.

There was water on the attic floor now, and Dad and Ralph wanted us to shift on to the roof. It didn't seem as if the flood could come any higher but if it did, they said we mustn't be trapped inside the attic. They had rigged up the trestle-table so it was half out of the attic window, and you could climb on it and step back on the roof at the gully between the two gables.

We all climbed out, and then they put the trestle across the gully of the roof for Mum and Gran to sit on. Ralph went back and got rugs and a cow-cover, and all the tinned food and the primus stove, and we made it like a little camp on top of our own roof. Dad pulled down the wireless aerial and made a kind of stay with it, and we draped the cow-cover over it because it was still raining, and sat there in that little tent.

But before I came out of the window I got the two little flat parcels that were my presents for Mum and Dad and brought them with me, tucked inside my shirt. Gran was rocking back and forth on the edge of the trestle-table, and Mum was comforting her.

When it was light we could see how bad the flood really was. The Hundred-Acre was like a big long island now, and it was just crowded with stock; there were horses and cows and sheep everywhere. They were all restless and the cows were bellowing and the sheep were bleating. They didn't race about, but they stood nervously, the horses holding their heads high. And in one corner there were three kangaroos, and a fox lying near them—all these animals, and none of them interfering with any of the others.

Out in the current there were dead animals floating down amongst the living. The trees that stood out of the water and the electric light poles were covered with spiders and little lizards and beetles; and some of the trees had snakes in the branches. There wasn't anything to do but just look at the water, and everything we looked at was something else to worry about.

The water had stopped coming up so fast, but it was still creeping up a little, about four inches every hour, Dad said.

Round about ten-o'clock we saw a little boat come around the farthest point upriver, about a mile away. It looked like the old boat Jim Tully used sometimes for fishing.

'Jim's mad to take that thing out,' Dad said.

But I could tell that it wasn't Jim Tully. And I knew who it was. 'It's Tommy,' I shouted. 'Tommy's coming.'

Nobody said anything, but they all stood up. Mum had her hand at her throat, and when the little boat twisted and swirled in the current she looked like death. But it came fast. It was half full of water when Tommy brought it up, heading it straight for the house. He wedged it in the gully right in front of the trestle-table, and stepped out on the roof.

'How's everybody?' he said.

'Could be worse,' Ralph told him.

'Why did you come, Tommy? It was risky,' Mum said.

'Thought I might be useful,' said Tommy. 'Things are bad. They don't expect it to go down for three days. I thought you might have trouble. The rescuers are out, but there's so much for them to do I thought it might be days before anyone got here. I've been on the road since the day before yesterday.'

'Tully might have needed his boat himself,' Dad said.

Tommy's face sobered. 'Bad news about the Tullys,' he said. 'Old Jim's gone. He didn't have time to make the house. He climbed the haystack, and the haystack went. No other news of

him. They brought in all the little Tullys, and Mrs Tully–got them off the roof.'

'Can we go back in the boat?' I asked him.

Tommy shook his head. 'Not a chance. That current must be running ten knots.'

'At least we can get over to the Hundred-Acre.' said Ralph.

'That was my idea too,' Tommy nodded.

It took hours to get over, one at a time with another one rowing; and then to bring over all the gear stacked on the roof. It was late afternoon when we had finished. There were aeroplanes flying over all the time, little spotter planes, and a seaplane, and two or three of the big Air Force bombers. I saw Tommy looking up at them.

We got a fire going when we reached the Hundred-Acre, and with the rain stopped we had a chance to get dry. The Peters family was there too. They had come over on a raft, the three of them, the father and mother and Shirley, who was only ten. And they didn't have anything to eat. We had to share some of our rugs and the tinned stuff with them.

Gran was feeling very sick. She was just lying wrapped up in rugs near the fire.

Only about half the Hundred-Acre was out of the water, and there were so many cattle it was already trampled and muddy, so there wasn't anything for the animals to eat. When it came night the cattle bellowed softly all the time. There were snakes and lizards everywhere; but we didn't kill them, we just left them.

'A lot of this stock won't last three days,' Dad said next morning. 'There's not going to be any feed when the water goes back, either. All that mud. They might have had a chance without these other animals.'

'While there's life, there's hope,' Ralph said cheerfully.

But Gran struggled in her blanket, and moved as though she wanted to sit up, and Mum ran to help her. She started to cough then, and Mum soothed her, and wanted to make her comfortable so she could lie down again; but Gran looked at Dad and said, 'Your father would have been ashamed to hear you, and on Christmas Day. Look you here,' she said, 'we spent our first Christmas under a tree, your father and I; in a wagon under a tree and little as we had, it was there to share. I never thought to hear

190

the day a lad of mine would grudge his neighbours a bit of help, and on Christmas Day.'

'It's not Christmas Day, Gran,' I told her. 'It's Christmas Eve. Christmas Day isn't till tomorrow.'

'It's Christmas Day,' she said, stubborn with her great age. 'It's Christmas Day for Ralph. It's Christmas Day whenever you're thinking of other people, and not of yourself. If you're not happy it's not a Christmas Day, and if you're thinking of yourself you're not so happy.' She looked confused, and pulled the blanket round herself, and lay down.

We had no water, and the brown flood water was thick and muddy. We were thirsty.

Then Mum found that Gran was fevered, and hot. We worried then. She was very old, and very tired; and she had had a hard time in the two nights—nearly three—of the flood.

But about ten o'clock that morning a Navy helicopter swung low over the hill, and we all jumped up and waved. The pilot had a loud-speaker attached to the helicopter somewhere, and his voice came booming down. 'If you can hang on another twenty-four hours hold up your right hands.'

I held up mine, and the others would have too, but Tommy yelled 'No', and pointed to Gran. Then we all pointed to Gran, and straight away the helicopter began to come down.

Tommy nudged me and shouted something, and his eyes were shining, but I didn't know what he was saying, for the noise was terrific under the rotor blades.

The helicopter settled down light and easy, and a man came out. They lifted Gran into it, her eyes big and wide as though she were frightened. And then Tommy said something to the man. They went off, the big egg-beater lifting into the air with a sort of a leap; and Tommy looking after it with his eyes lifted.

Dad was happier now. 'That's one worry off our minds.'

'Worries never last long,' Mum told him.

'Neither does tobacco,' he said. 'I'd sure feel happier if I could fill the old pipe.' Dad had no tobacco in his pipe. So I felt under my shirt for his present. I pulled it out and gave it to him.

'Merry Christmas, Dad,' I said. 'I wanted to keep it for the right day, but I guess you might like it today.'

He looked at me and said, 'Oh, Dave' in a soft kind of way. He

191

unwrapped it, and it was a new leather tobacco pouch. I'd wondered in the store whether to spend more money and fill it for him, and then I thought it would look better filled, and thank goodness I'd bought the tobacco as well.

'It doesn't look like Christmas, but I think there's a feel of it in the air,' Dad said. He picked me up and swung me high, same as he used to do when I was a little kid. I thought of something else and I asked him: 'Dad, can we have a Christmas tree for tomorrow?'

He laughed and looked around. There weren't any real she-oaks on top of the hill, of course; but there was a little gum-tree, the biggest of a group, about ten feet high.

'We could use that one,' I said.

'We haven't anything to put on it, son,' Dad said.

But we didn't have the tree in the tub any more, and we didn't have the Christmas bush; and there weren't going to be any presents, only what I still had for Mum; and there wouldn't be any Christmas dinner or anything; and suddenly they all seemed to see it my way; and we began to get the tree ready for Christmas, as well as we could. We cut away all the other saplings and just left this one gum-tree standing by itself; and it was a lovely little tree, with the first blossoms it had ever had crowning it.

We just stood and looked at it then. There was some horse-hair caught in the fence, and Dad said, 'You're not going to get my tobacco back to hang on it. Because it tastes so good. But I'll hang this instead, just to show it should have been there.'

And he tied the wrapping paper into a little bundle and hung it on the end of one of the branches. And I hung Mum's present on another. Then everybody tied handkerchiefs and bits of stones and sticks and things everywhere; and it looked really a bit like a Christmas tree, even if it was a kind of Christmas tree that nobody had ever seen before; and every stick and stone stood for a present from one to the other; and we invited the Peters family to share the tree, and they hung things on it too.

Late in the afternoon one of the big Air Force bombers came over and circled the hill. The back door in the fuselage was open, and Tommy ran to Dad, very excited.

'Move the stock back,' he yelled. 'It's the feed.' Dad, Ralph and I ran at the stock, shouting and waving our arms, trying to send them to the other end of the hill so there would be a clear patch left at our end. The bomber had circled and was coming back.

'I asked the helicopter pilot,' Tommy said. 'I told him we needed stock food. This is the feed arriving.'

The bomber was overhead now, and three bales of hay came flying from the open door. It circled again; three more bales came out. I saw the third lot come all the way down. I saw the bale hit the Christmas tree and break it off; break it right down. It snapped right off into the ground.

The last bundle was a bundle of blankets, and in the blankets, wrapped up, were parcels of food, and tablets to purify the flood water for drinking; and dozens of little things we hadn't known we'd needed.

'What about the Air Force now?' said Tommy.

Dad put his pipe in his mouth and said, 'You win. A fellow can't be expected to know what he's talking about all the time, can he?'

Ralph was looking at all the things wrapped in the blankets.

'Plenty of fol-de-rols to hang on the Christmas tree now,' he said.

'But there isn't any tree,' I told him.

I felt mighty sick about it too. I wanted that tree; and that old bale of hay could have landed almost anywhere else in the Hundred-Acre. Ralph put his arm round me and said, 'Gee, Dave, that's the worst kind of luck.'

'It doesn't matter,' I said. 'I'd rather the stock had the hay.' And just then I remembered, and I rushed to the tree where it was lying in the ground. And my present for Mum, the little flat bottle of French perfume, was smashed.

And then I started to cry just like a little kid. I thought I was too old to cry; and I reckon I'll remember it because that's the last time I'm ever going to cry; but I couldn't help it then. I was crying when Mum came over and I showed her the broken bottle. She picked up the stopper.

'I'm going to keep this anyway,' she said. 'It'll make the nicest kind of remembering present. You know, I'd have used the scent, and that would have been that; but the stopper I'll put away and keep it always. It's the only thing I'll ever have that will really remind me of this Christmas, and how we all were.' It sounded silly, but there was a kind of sense in what she was saying, and I listened.

'Everything's going to be all right, you know,' she said. 'Tommy's going to join the Air Force and Dad's going to be proud of him; and you and Ralph and all of us are going to be happy. It's going to be a really happy Christmas for us all.'

Dad was standing near, and he had his back to us, but I think he was listening.

'There wasn't any roof for the Babe in the Manger; his home was somewhere else, and his gifts came from strangers, just like ours have,' Mum said. 'But that's the Christmas everyone all over the world remembers.'

And it might sound silly; but when I look back on it now, that Christmas we spent in the flood last year was the happiest Christmas ever.

A Christmas Eve

Harry Macfie

The full moon shone silvery white and the shadows of the tall dry aspens made fantastic patterns on the sparkling white snow. On the opposite shore the fir trees stood in close formation and threw dark shadows far out on to the ice, which rumbled and cracked continually under several feet of thick snow. The terror of the hares, the great wood owl with its horn-like tufts of feathers, uttered its weird cry from some fir-top over by the falls, now almost frozen up. The trees cracked in the fearful cold; the sound rang through the night like shots.

It was Christmas Eve. Our little log cabin on the shore of Star Lake was almost buried in snow. Smoke, and now and then a spark, rose from the low stone-faced chimney straight to the star-strewn sky. Five pairs of snow-shoes stood in the snow outside one main wall, and a long toboggan, with its upward-tilted front, leaned against the roof. Bill's and Jack's Mackenzie dogs, tired after their sixty-miles' journey, lay dug down into the snow. Fantastic shadows from the blazing wood fire inside danced on the ice-covered window.

Tom Moore, the old one-eyed trapper who had come to us on snow-shoes through endless woods, had brewed his strongest punch that evening. The brew stood on the hearth, hissing gently from the heat of the glowing fire.

One old song had followed another, and as I stood outside in the cold Christmas night after giving an extra feed to the dogs—which had crept back into their holes in the snow and hidden their muzzles under their bushy tails, pleased and contented with the tit-bits they had received—I heard Tom start that beautiful old song 'My Old Kentucky Home'. The melody was muffled by the wooden walls of the hut, but I joined in the refrain. As I did so I thought I heard the sharp crack of a rifle a long way off. I stopped singing and listened. Again I thought I

195

heard a shot in the direction of Hawk Lake, then another and yet another. But who would be shooting now, at night, and at what?

The shots might possibly have been fired at wolves, but no one lived in that direction except old Corbet and his Mary, and that was twenty miles away. A shot could not be heard so far even in that degree of cold. It must have been the trees on the other side of the lake cracking in the frost. I went in, however, and told the others what I thought I had heard. When I opened the door the cold rushed in and formed a sort of white mist over the moose hides on the floor.

We all went out into the night and listened, but we heard nothing but the rumbling of the ice and the cracking of the trees. I must have been mistaken. We went in again and enjoyed the warmth and Tom's punch.

We sat up late, talking over experiences and happenings in the wilds. Smoke rose from our pipes and the fading glow of the fire spread a ruddy sheen over the round barked logs and weather-beaten faces. By degrees the conversation died down, and we went to bed, rolling ourselves up in our hare-skin robes.

Now and then a flame sprang up from some resinous knot, shone for a moment, then died away. The hoar-frost grew thicker on the small window-panes. Outside it was growing colder. There was a rumbling from the ice on the lake. Or was it shots I thought I heard in my sleep, over from Hawk Lake?

Christmas morning was clear, and a pale sun, with no warmth in it, tried to rise over the ridge to eastward. But we could see nothing more than a lightening of the sky. The cold was terrible and was becoming more and more severe, but indoors we were warm and comfortable. Hard-frozen meat hung in large portions in the shed behind the wall, and there was no lack of other provisions.

I could not forget the shots I thought I had heard, and decided to take the dogs and drive over to see old Corbet on the north shore of Hawk Lake.

The five big wolf-dogs were soon harnessed, and we set off at full gallop down on to the snow covering of the ice; here small fir twigs marked the well-trodden snow-shoe trail which now lay covered by a couple of inches of snow after the last fall. It was too cold to drive in the toboggan, so I held on to one of the lines and ran behind the team.

The crossing of the lake did not take long, and we were soon in the forest, where the path ran along the now almost silent torrent. Then we went down a slope beside the falls, and so came down to Hawk Lake, whose white surface stretched for miles from east to west. The running had warmed me up, and I continued the journey across the lake alternately riding and running.

The hoar-frost hung white from the heads and chests of the dogs, their breath issued from their mouths in thick clouds, and the tinkle of the little bells on the leader's harness was faint as the result of ice forming on the metal. Before us the white surface lay untouched; only the sprigs of fir showed where our road ran; but behind us our own fresh tracks were plainly visible in the pale winter daylight.

When I had been driving for a little while I discovered a trail which crossed our road at right angles. At first I could not see what had made the trail, but when I reached the place where it crossed our path, I found it was the trail of a man plunging forward through the deep snow without snow-shoes, dragging a toboggan.

The trail wound forward across the snow-field towards the shore where the pines stood weighed down with snow, in towards what remained of old Pete's hut.

I halted the team, put on the snow-shoes which lay lashed to the toboggan, and set off along the trail. The snow-shoes' cross-binding of raw hide left an oblong impression on the snow behind each step, and the dogs followed my tracks towards the shore.

Here the man had sat on the toboggan, and the trail went on. I followed, and could see when still a long way off how he had crawled in the snow up the slope below the cabin. The toboggan was still standing on the shore.

I halted my team and went up the slope alone. The dogs lifted their frosty heads to the sky and howled.

The trail led under the young trees over to the big fir. The man had stood there some time by the hillock and then gone on to the little hut.

Half the roof had fallen in, but one side of it still clung firmly to the ridge, and on this still stood the long white row of grinning bears' skulls which Pete had set there long ago. The snow had formed a high forehead on each skull, giving it a grotesque appearance.

The trail ran forward to the door, where the mark of a hand showed that the man had supported himself against a log in the wall, then led round the corner of the hut.

The man was lying dead by the ashes of a log fire. His stiff frozen fingers still held the rifle pointed at his head, which had frozen hard into the bloody snow. His bare feet were chalk-white; one moccasin lay burnt by the fire, the other in the snow close by, from which empty cartridge cases also projected.

I went down on to the ice again and fetched a small grey worn blanket, which was lying on his toboggan, to cover him with. He had had no provisions with him; a few white beans in a cloth bag, a small piece of meat and a frozen crust of bread, that was all.

He must have known Pete and had come to look for him. He had made his way laboriously across the lake, starving and with frozen feet. Why had he left his little outfit on the ice and taken only the rifle with him when he crawled up through the snow to Pete's hut?

I could guess the tragedy in part. When he found that the cabin was deserted and in ruins, and Pete not there, he had crept around, gathered a little fuel and made a fire, at which he had tried to thaw his frozen feet. Then he had fired a few shots to summon help.

When the little fuel he had collected was finished, cold and death had crept nearer and nearer in the Christmas night. Then he preferred to put an end to his sufferings by shooting himself.

I walked along to the big fir out on the point, where a little cross, discoloured by wind and weather, stood above a mound in the snow. Here lay the old trapper and bear-hunter Pete Vergeland, and it was nearly two years since we had dug his grave out there on the point.

Old Pete was born in Norway very many years ago and had come to Canada as a little boy. The last time we saw Pete alive was when we found him in the forest by a little stream where he used to have his bear-traps in spring. A dead bear lay there with one foot in a trap, an axe-wound in its head and several knife-thrusts in its chest, and beneath its claws, Pete, terribly injured and dying.

It was not hard to guess what had happened. Pete had approached the trapped bear to kill it with his axe; his rifle stood against a tree a little way off. Pete had been over-confident that time; his blow had been misdirected, the bear had seized him and they had fought out their last battle alone. We could do nothing

199

for him; he died while we were carrying him down to the lake.

So Pete lay here at rest under his white mound, and up there, behind the hut, his friend or enemy lay frozen stiff with his head shot to pieces, covered by a worn grey blanket. And upon the sagging ridge of the roof was a long row of grinning bear-skulls.

The dogs were eager to be off, and, leaving the small and solitary toboggan on the ice, I drove out again to the winter trail and on northwards across the lake towards old Corbet's cabin on the headland.

The smoke could be seen rising from the iron chimney a long way off. I met old Mary coming down from the hill dragging a load of dry wood. She was wading in the snow up to her knees. We went in to see the old man. As usual, he was lying on his back in bed among the blankets, smoking and composing one of his everlasting poems, with the stump of a pencil in one hand and a scrap of paper in the other.

Corbet and Mary had lived there as long as anyone could remember. Corbet had a long white beard and talked an educated English which years in the wilds had not changed. He received an annual remittance from the old country. Once a year he and Mary paddled, or, to be more correct, Mary paddled him to the nearest railway station, Ingolf, which was really only a water tank and telegraph office. They got into the train there and went into Rat Portage, where Corbet drew his money against a receipt. They bought necessaries, returned by train to Ingolf, and Mary paddled him home, so that for another year he could continue to write poetry at his ease. The old man had done this for years and years.

It was fearfully hot inside the cabin. The little metal stove was red-hot and half the pipe too. Feeble sunlight seeped in through the low window, and on the sill stood a few languishing plants in jam jars. Every inch of the walls was covered with pasted-up newspaper cuttings.

Mary gave us tea and freshly baked cakes. I told Corbet and Mary about the stranger whom I had found out on Pete's point. They had not seen anything of him.

The short day was approaching its end. The sky was a cold green with a faint red tinge over the wooded islets out in the narrows to southward, and the snow on Hawk Lake was shot with blue.

It was time for me to make a start, and the dogs, which had had a much needed rest of an hour or two, were eager to run home.

The old man was delighted at having something new to write about, and he had already composed the first line of his poem about the two dead men over there on the headland.

Mary came out to see me off. I knelt down on the toboggan and gave the word to the dogs.

The long whip-lash cracked over the leading dog, and the team sped away over the plain, where the shadows of the trail fell blue-black on the snow-field.

It was dark already when we swept past Pete's point, but soon we had only the ice of our own lake to cross. There in the creek twinkled the light from our cabin window. The dogs pulled at their harness and galloped along the trail. Their comrades at home howled and whined as I drove up the slope from the shore and stopped outside the door. The dogs were unharnessed and they rolled in the snow; then they were fed.

Inside the cabin it was pleasant and warm and Christmas-like, and Tom had brewed a fresh bowl of punch. I related my experiences, and we all wondered who the stranger was and why he had been looking for old Pete.

We went there next morning. The old man lay as he had lain the day before, under his worn grey blanket, glittering with frost. None of us had seen him before, and he had nothing on him which could give any indication as to who he was.

The ground was frozen hard and deep, and the blows of pick-axes and the rattle of spades rang out dully. At last we had the grave dug and laid him in it, wrapped in the old blanket. We laid his rifle beside him, and filled up the hole with earth and snow.

Pete's little mound is a short way off.

Here the old men lie on the headland in Hawk Lake, and whether friendship or hate brought them together at last is and will remain one of the unsolved mysteries of the wild.

Then we christened the headland 'Dead Men's Point'.

The Charcoal Burner

Gerald Kersh

Glaring with red eyes that bulged out of blackened orbits, the charcoal burner looked more like a devil than a man. His beard, if it had been washed, would have been white; but it was so full of black dust that the fires of hell might have scorched it. The lost traveller was appalled, for a moment, by the inhuman ferocity of the old man's appearance. But the storm was rising and, between his shoulderblades, he felt a spatter of hard snow–to employ an image belonging to our times, here were the tracer bullets of the blizzard finding their target.

'Let me in!' cried the traveller. 'For God's sake, let me in!'

'Hey there, Hektor!' shouted the old man; and there appeared a great black-and-grey dog, three-parts wolf, hideously fanged.

In a breaking voice, the wayfarer said: 'For the love of God, man, let me in! All I ask is to lie by your fire. A bit of bread . . . an onion . . . anything. I will pay you well. Here—' His hands were very cold, but after some fumbling he found a large silver coin–his fingers were too numb to take hold of a smaller one–and offered it.

The old charcoal burner snatched the coin, tasted it, bit it, put it away under his rags, and growled: 'I thought you were another of these tax-gatherers. Even so, I don't like company. You can come in, if you like, seeing as you pay your way; which is a devil of a long sight more than most people do. . . . Down, Hektor! . . . Ah, yes, sir, you may well look! Hektor's mother was a grey wolf. If I snapped my fingers once, he'd pin you; if I snapped them twice, he'd tear your throat out.' Maliciously, the charcoal burner extended a blackened hand and took a pinch of air between thumb and second finger.

'Don't do it!' cried the visitor, watching the dog who, crouching for a spring, was growling deep in his throat.

The old man said: 'You can sit by my fire, if you like. Since you've paid for it, you can have some soup.'

'Thank you,' said the traveller, shaking snow out of his fur cloak and coming through a stinging fog of stinking smoke towards the fire. 'Some soup, yes, and shelter until daybreak. Do you happen to have something strong to drink?'

'Plum brandy–if you can pay for it,' said the old man.

'Why,' cried the traveller, 'I have already paid you more than you could earn in three months! Get out your plum brandy this instant, you surly dog!'

'Speaking of dog...' said the old man, and held up conjoined thumb and second finger. Hektor snarled, crouching again. The traveller found a small coin this time, which he gave to the old man who, then, pulled as it were from out of the smoke that filled the hovel a crockery jar half full of something that had the perfume of an autumnal orchard delicately flavoured with wood smoke. Of this the traveller drank. The charcoal burner drank, too. Scratching the place where he had put his money–under his left armpit–he said: 'You are some kind of a clerk?'

'That is right,' said the traveller.

'I can tell from your dress,' said the old man, 'and by the way you carry your sword. What is more, your cloak is of fox fur. You must be a middling high-up kind of clerk; otherwise you'd be wearing coney, or mole-skin, at the best... not wolfskin–oh no! There's more warmth in that than any amount of foxes. But that's fit only for the likes of me.... Vanity, vanity! Go on, have some more plum brandy, and eat your soup. If you want bread, you can whistle for it, because I haven't got any.'

Warmed by the fire and the plum brandy, the visitor said: 'You are a charcoal burner, I take it, my friend?'

'How d'you think I got so black? Weaving silk? Making tapestry? It isn't a clean trade, mister, charcoal burning. If you don't believe me, you try it and see! Have some more plum brandy, if you like.... Oho! Particular, are you? Go on, then–wipe the jar on your sleeve. Is it my fault I follow a dirty trade, and get all black? Drink, and pass the jar.'

The visitor said: 'I see that you are a misanthrope, my friend. That means to say, that you do not like your fellow creatures.'

The charcoal burner replied: 'I have too much to do to like my fellow creatures. All I know is the forest: out with my axe and cut and cut and cut–wood, wood, wood. Then, make my stack, light my fires, and wait and wait and wait. Fill my baskets, hump 'em

into town, sell the charcoal for what I can get... and back again! Cut and burn and carry, carry and burn and cut.... I like the little trees. Tell you something—I'd as soon hew down a man as a sweet little tree.' The charcoal burner drank more plum brandy. 'By killing the things I love, to warm the creatures I don't like—that's how I live.'

'That is life, friend,' said the traveller.

'I know, and you can keep it.'

'But, my friend, judging by your accent, you are not from these parts, surely?'

'No, I'm from over the Frontier. Ran away. Too much taxes. I was born and bred over there by St. Agnes's. I was comfortable enough, but they won't leave a man alone. What was it you called me just now—miserope?'

'*Misanthrope*, my friend; which means one who dislikes his fellow creatures.'

'Well, you are not far wrong, you know. The more I've seen of men, the more I love my dog. I wasn't always like this, though, was I, Hektor?' The wolf-dog growled as it were in assent. The old man took another drink of plum brandy and continued:

'When I lived over by St. Agnes's, I used to be a good-natured fellow enough, until my woman died in child-bed, and after that I kept myself to myself—cut my wood, charred my wood, sold my charcoal, made ends meet. Earned enough to keep me and my dogs. Twenty years ago this was, mind you.

'I don't mind telling you that if you hadn't shoved a little ready money through the door tonight I'd have let you go out into the storm, and be damned to you. But in those days I was full of good nature. This was in Hektor's Grandmother's time. She was having a litter just about then. Her husband, the dog, was called Kuli—great big red beast—could pin a wild pig by the ear or pull down a wolf. More than half wolf himself—couldn't even bark—could only howl.... Have some more plum brandy? No? Well, if you won't, I will.

'One night, in a crackling frost, with the snow knee-deep, Kuli starts howling. "That means strangers," I says to myself. Now the nearest fellow human being lived a league or two away, by the palace, and they wasn't likely to come and visit the likes of me. So I calls Kuli, and gets my axe, and covers my ears with my cap, and I looks out. Well, up on the hill (I'm in the valley by the forest, d'you see) somebody is waving a lantern and crying for help. I says to Kuli: "Go, mark 'em, boy; mark 'em Kuli!" And off Kuli goes, loping like a wolf through the snow. I follow in Kuli's tracks, and they lead me to an old gentleman and a boy lost in a snowdrift. The old gentleman is carrying under his cloak a kind of bundle. The boy is shivering in his shoes, empty-handed. The old gentleman says: "Lead me to St. Agnes's." In those days, I'd do anything for anybody. D'you follow me?

'"A matter of five hundred paces," I says, "Follow me, gentlemen." D'you follow me?

'So they follow me. The boy falls down. The old gentleman has his hands full with his parcels, so I slings the young 'un across my shoulders, and Kuli leads us back to my hut.

'I'm not a rich man, never have been—if I was, you understand, I wouldn't be burning charcoal in the bitter forest and coughing black. All the same, I always make ends meet—' the charcoal burner put the tips of his forefingers together, '—like *that*. One thing I always have in my hut, and that is, a good fire. Well, that year hadn't been a good one. Still, I had soup in the pot. For the sake of Christian charity—in those days, I believed in Christian charity—I chucked in my last chunk of bacon, and rubbed the boy's frozen feet with snow (*he* would have thawed them directly at the fire!) and old Kuli licked them just as the dog in the Bible licked the sores of Lazarus. . . . If you ask me, Kuli licked the boy's feet for the sake of the salt. But when the old man saw this, he burst into tears. Proud and humble, both at the same time.

'Then I put the soup into my one bowl, and they ate. Oh, but how that boy could tuck the grub away! The old man had the spoon. He sniffed and he sipped, he sipped and he sniffed, and he said: "What do you put in this, my poor man?" I told him—a bit of bacon, a bit of goat, a few roots. Wild garlic, essential; but first of all throw into your pot some pig's fat and half a handful of flour. "Fry the flour in the fat until it is brown. Then, toss in half a handful of the fruit of the sweet pepper tree, dried and ground up," I told him, "but not with the seeds. They'll burn your tongue. Add water—a little to begin with—stir it up, and after that sling in what you like. Anything goes."

'By this time, the rime was melted off his cloak, and I could see that he was dressed in sable and ermine. No doubt about it, he was a Somebody. I had a little bit of plum brandy left in the house, so I

offered it. I make it myself. You've tasted it. It's not bad, is it?...
Well, the old gentleman drank, and so did the young 'un. At last,
the old one got up and said: "Now I see how the Poor live." The
frost had melted in his beard, and turned to water. He shook it out
into my fire, where it hissed. Then he looked me up and down and
said:

'"I came here, my man, to bring you gifts in honour of the
season of the year... a haunch of venison, some wine, and fuel.
The meat and the wine, unfortunately, were lost when my page
Prokop dropped them into a snowdrift. The Christmas fuel,
however, I have with me. Take it!" And he threw down three
little pine logs. "Not that you appear to need it," he said, "the heat
in your hovel is suffocating.... Have you a timber-drag?"

'As if he didn't know: a charcoal burner without a timber-drag,
I ask you! So I nodded, and he said: "Take my page and me home,
fellow." And what could I do but obey the old beard, since he was
King Vaclav–the one they made the ballad about–the old man
they call Good King Wenceslas? The following spring, he took a
mistress from Wallachia, and wow, but she stung him to rights! A
castle, no less, and three thousand acres o' fat land! Light head and
heavy purse make light purse and heavy head. He remembered,
then, how well the Poor live–meaning me–and slapped on such a
heavy tax that I fled the country.

'Can you wonder that I do not welcome visitors at this time of
the year?'

Drowsily, the traveller shook his head. Then he nodded. Just
before he fell asleep he heard the old charcoal burner grumble:
'The very idea of the old fool, bringing *me* pine logs....'

Lost Leader

Dennis Hamley

The timbers of the longship had rotted away centuries ago. One day, archaeologists would dig into the grassy surface and expose the marks they had left in the soil. One day, the gold-embossed shield and armour, the helmet with the golden boar's crest and the mighty sword, silver-inlaid and studded with garnets, would sparkle under a museum's careful lighting.

But not yet. Now they were dark as the darkness of the burial chamber they were placed in to accompany the High King on his last journey.

The High King, however, must have forgotten them. The burial chamber was empty.

The Mounds overlooked the town. You would have a four mile walk from them, down the shallow sloping grass, past the gravel workings, across fields and through woods until you reached the first housing estates. On this particular day you would see Christmas trees through front windows and holly wreaths on doors, the decorated High Street and coloured lights on the big tree in the Market Square. And you might turn down the road where the Willis family lived.

Dusk settled on a damp, muggy Christmas Eve. The last postman had long gone home. But one figure still flitted from door to door with notices to deliver. He was from the Footpath Preservation Society, which each week stamped in a body over little-used rights of way, and he was spreading details of the annual Boxing Day walk, a convivial wander which would end with beer, wine, and mince pies in the secretary's house. He was not due to go to the Willises.

Yet, somehow, one of his notices became detached from his bundle. A light wind blew it–a piece of unnoticed litter–to wiry,

209

alien hands which were waiting. And later the same wiry hands pushed at the Willis letter box. A wisp of paper floated to the doormat. The messenger, fleet of foot, darted up the road.

'What time are they arriving?' asked Mr Willis.

'Sylvie said to expect them when we see them,' said his wife. 'Matthew, leave that trifle alone.'

'I know she's your sister and she's bringing her new boyfriend,' said Mr Willis. 'But this is going a bit far, isn't it?'

The table groaned under the weight of sausages, chicken drumsticks, quiche, bowls of salad, the trifle Matthew had craftily raided, and exotic-looking gateaux defrosting after their previous existence at Bejams.

'We must give a good impression. This means a lot to Sylvie. It might be her chance at last,' said Mrs Willis.

'Or her last chance,' said Mr Willis. 'Look at all the men she's brought here. Superman 3 the lot of them. Now where are they?'

'What about the great TV star?' said Stephanie. 'A small part on a Building Society commercial.'

'And the professional footballer who was going to win the World Cup for us,' said Matthew. 'Turned out he played for Stockport County Reserves.'

'It's true,' sighed Mrs Willis. 'All Sylvie's swans are geese.'

The doorbell rang.

'That's them,' said Mrs Willis. 'Stephanie and Matthew, go and let them in, please.'

Sister and brother saw two misty shapes through the frosted glass of the front door. The smaller one they knew; they could make out Sylvie's black hair, dark eyes and red lips. The other was huge and indistinct.

Stephanie opened the door. Immediately she was enveloped by Sylvie's arms, a strong smell of Chanel and a vibrant, carrying voice.

'Hal-*lo*, my dear. How *mar*-vellous to see you. *Hap*-py Christmas.'

Matthew couldn't escape the same treatment. Then Sylvie turned on their parents. Eventually she released them and stood before the front door like a ringmaster.

'Now,' she said. 'I want you all to meet Oliver.'

Oliver stepped inside.

The Willis family gasped.

Oliver was nearly seven feet tall and broad-shouldered with it. He wore a sheepskin coat. His blond hair was thick and curly; a square beard jutted forward. His face had an open-air ruddiness and his hands were like legs of lamb.

'Happy Christmas to you all,' he said in a voice which reverberated round the hallway. 'I'm so very pleased to meet you.'

'Get the cases and presents out of the car, please, Oliver,' said Sylvie.

Oliver lumbered out to the red Metro parked outside.

'We came in my car,' said Sylvie. 'He's the guest, so I wouldn't let him use his Jag.'

'Go and help, Matthew,' said Mum.

Too late. Oliver was back already, bearing suitcases and Christmas-wrapped parcels as if they were matchboxes.

'There's something stuck to your shoe,' said Stephanie.

A piece of white paper extended from his heel. He picked it up and looked at it.

'Addressed to "The Occupier",' he said. 'Someone put it through your letterbox.'

Stephanie took it and smoothed it out. Faint letters done on an old ink duplicator crossed the paper like birds' footprints over snow. She read aloud.

> 'Footpath Society. Boxing Day walk. Get rid of your Christmas hangover. Eight mile walk in good company. Circular tour via the Mounds. Meet Market Square 10.30. Rights of Way are extinguished every day. The countryside is *yours*. Walk the paths and keep the Right of Way. JOIN THE SOCIETY.'

'Throw it away,' said Mum.

'No,' said Dad. 'It makes sense.'

'I'll be there,' said Oliver. 'Where do I put this lot?'

By nine o'clock, Mr Willis's buffet supper was cleaned out. Oliver had eaten three-quarters of it and drunk rather more. 'Quite magnificent,' he said, several times. Apart from one ruminative belch he seemed none the worse for wear. Stephanie and Matthew watched him, fascinated.

'I'll help wash up,' said Sylvie as Mum went to the kitchen.

'So will I,' said Dad.

After a moment, Stephanie and Matthew joined them, leaving Oliver changing channels on the television set as if he owned it.

'Well, what do you think?' said Sylvie excitedly.

Dad cleared his throat.

'What does he do for a living, Sylvie?' he said.

'He's a *hero*,' said Sylvie.

'A what?' said Dad.

'Isn't that enough?' said Sylvie.

'He's in the SAS,' said Matthew.

'Or the IRA,' said Stephanie.

'Perhaps he's a double-agent,' said Mum.

'Is being a hero a paying game, then?' said Dad.

'Oliver never thinks about money,' said Sylvie.

'He can't do too badly if he's got a Jag,' said Mum.

'I wouldn't trust him further than I could throw him,' said Dad.

Sylvie's big, dark eyes brimmed with tears.

'HE...IS...A...HERO,' she sobbed and ran out of the kitchen and upstairs.

'Now look what you've done,' said Mum.

Oliver poked his huge blond head round the door.

'Sylvie a bit upset, is she?' he said. 'Not to worry. I'll go and calm her down.'

'There,' said Mum. 'He may be just what Sylvie needs.'

'Pull the other one,' said Dad.

'What are we going to *do* with him?' said Mum.

It was four o'clock on Christmas afternoon. Oliver, in the best armchair, was replete and expansive.

'You know,' he said as he smoked a cigar and drank Dad's whisky, 'Christmas is only an excuse for a big feed-up.'

Stephanie and Matthew couldn't take their eyes off him.

'Yes,' he went on. 'Long before Christmas came, there was the great winter feast. When you ate everything you could before it went bad and lived off your fat till spring came.'

Sylvie watched him adoringly.

'Those were the days,' he said. 'The great feast in the King's Hall. Inside, warmth and jollity; outside, cold, darkness and monsters prowling.'

He sipped his whisky.

'I sometimes think I'm out of place in the twentieth century,' he said. 'I belong in a more *expansive* time. When there weren't all these curbs on what you can do and what you can't. When you owed your duty to your king and that was all you need worry about.'

Three pairs of eyes continued to watch him.

'I should have been a Saxon King or a Danish War-Lord. With salt spray in my face as forty oars carried my longship over the wave road. I should have lived then. Not in this silly, pussy-footing time.'

In the kitchen Mum was nearly in tears.

'I bought a twenty-pound turkey,' she said. 'It should have lasted a week. And look at it.'

The pathetic skeleton resembled a picture in the *Beano*.

'And the Christmas pudding went in two mouthfuls,' she continued.

Dad had his own woes.

'All the whisky's gone. He drank a party can of bitter all by himself. And look at this.' He pointed indignantly at a shapeless object. 'A three-litre box of French Red.'

The empty container had collapsed and the tiny tap crept forlornly back inside.

'What are we going to *do*?' said Mum again.

213

'And the worst was when you were out of the room,' said Dad. 'The telly was on. And he *belched* all the way through the Queen. He stood up for the National Anthem. And that nearly shook the house down. Like Vesuvius erupting.'

'I was thinking of cold turkey, jacket potato, and salad for Boxing Day lunch,' said Mum. 'But he's cleaned us out.'

'I'll have a word with that Sylvie,' said Dad.

'Still,' said Mum, 'the Patels' shop opens tomorrow. I'll get a tinned ham. Three tinned hams.'

Sylvie entered the kitchen.

'Look how much your man's eaten,' said Dad.

'Yes, I know,' Sylvie breathed. 'Isn't he *wonderful?*'

'Please,' said Mum. 'Make sure he goes on that walk tomorrow morning while I stock up.'

Oliver was still holding forth from his armchair.

'That would have been my scene. Remember Beowulf. A great banquet in Hrothgar's Hall. The monster Grendel is dead. The warriors feast on whole boars roasted at a time. Gallons of fresh-brewed ale. Tales of the great heroes of old. Fighting men joined in brotherhood. That would have been the time for me.'

He lifted his glass as if toasting some invisible warrior.

'Yes,' he said. 'Hrothgar's Hall is my spiritual home.'

Sylvie entered and spoke to the open-mouthed Matthew and Stephanie. 'Oliver wants to go on tomorrow's walk,' she said. 'Why don't you take him? I can spare him for a few hours.'

'Excellent,' cried Oliver. In the kitchen the Willises drew heartfelt sighs of relief.

Boxing Day stayed dark and mild. The ground was soft underfoot. Thirty people gathered in the Market Square. When Stephanie, Matthew and Oliver arrived, a thin man clothed as if to conquer Everest was addressing them.

'Very pleasing to see new faces this morning. I shall lead. We walk four miles to the Mounds and four back by a different route. We may have to clear paths and cut wire on the way. Follow me.'

A straggly crocodile shuffled down the High Street.

'The Mounds are big grassy lumps,' said Matthew.

'There may be ancient treasure under them,' said Stephanie. 'There's going to be a dig there soon.'

'I know,' said Oliver.

Matthew and Stephanie thought they were last in the crocodile. But as they took the road out of town they became aware of measured footsteps behind them. They looked back.

Two blond men in red anoraks, waterproof trousers and fell boots walked side by side. They carried strong wooden staves in their hands. They looked like identical twins as they marched together in perfect step five paces behind–awesomely, like bodyguards.

Some of the walkers complained as they turned down yet another road of semi-detached houses.

'I didn't expect a tour of the housing estates,' said one.

'Patience,' cried the leader and led them over a stile at the road's end. When all were across, the party looked back at the hedge and forward to the distant woods. The town might not have been there.

'Straight across the field,' said the leader. 'You can't see the path but there's one on the map. The farmer keeps ploughing it up.'

One or two newcomers looked worried. Suddenly, Oliver took the lead, plunging over the ploughed earth.

'The shortest way is the only way,' he shouted.

'This is very naughty,' said the leader when they reached the woods on the other side. 'The owner has put barbed wire across the fence. He has no right. The maps show a right of way.'

He produced a pair of wire-cutters. The newcomers looked even more doubtful. Oliver spoke again.

'Quite right. Cut the wire. The only rights to be respected are the rights of conquest.'

The two blond walkers moved closer to Oliver.

The party filed through dank woods; more wire was cut to get out. Then across and round more fields until a woeful sight appeared–a great, bare gash in the ground. Far below, on a roughly tarred road, stood excavators, empty lorries and a deserted Portakabin.

'Gravel workings,' said the leader. 'They'll make good the landscape but we must protect the path across it.' He led them down into thick, cloying mud.

'It's worse than the Somme,' said someone.

'You're right,' cried Oliver delightedly. 'It is.'

He started into the mud as if he had won the Battle of the Somme single-handed. The two blond walkers followed him, one

215

on each side. A secret look of recognition seemed to pass between the three.

Stephanie and Matthew now nearly gave up. When they reached the far side of the workings their boots weighed like lead and yellow mud clung up to their knees. The party huddled together, inadequately scraping mud off, too exhausted to be rebellious. Except for Oliver and his new companions, who were spotless.

The leader allowed rest. Above them now was a grass-covered shallow slope, deserted except for a few far-off sheep. At the top were the Mounds.

'Ready?' called the leader.

On they went. By now, Matthew and Stephanie felt Oliver had deserted them in favour of his minders as they approached the enigmatic grassy bumps. The sky was darkening; the atmosphere strangely heavy; the footpath walkers grimly silent. An odd air of expectancy hung round them.

They had arrived. The leader stopped by the largest mound— eighty feet long like a gigantic half-submerged green sausage. He seemed to want to talk about the Mounds, to speculate on what unknown thing might lie inside. But, though his mouth opened and closed, no words came.

The sky was at its blackest. Oliver and his bodyguard stood together, facing the side of the largest mound. There was a sudden

growl of unseasonal thunder. A second later, the Mounds were lit up with a slow sheet of lightning.

Afterwards, everybody agreed exactly on what they had seen.

In front of the three men, a black cleft opened up in the side of the Mound. The three, resolutely, unflinchingly, walked inside. When the lightning died away, the walkers saw the grassy side of the Mound was untouched—as it had been for fourteen centuries.

And that was not all. Matthew and Stephanie were sure of this; so was every hard-bitten adult there. Oliver and his bodyguard were not wearing modern walking gear. Instead, armour and suits of chainmail flashed from them. They carried long, iron-tipped spears. They wore shining helmets, Oliver's crested in gold with the sign of a great boar. And they disappeared into the Mound with the air of returning majesty.

'It's all true, every word,' insisted Stephanie.

They were back home. The footpath walkers had run headlong to town and the police station. Here the disbelieving desk sergeant had threatened to do them all for drunk and disorderly. So they crept home to think.

Mr and Mrs Willis were doubtful. But Sylvie, in Oliver's armchair, looked ecstatic, transfigured.

'Oh, Oliver,' she breathed. 'I knew it all along. The *hero*.'

'Come off it Sylvie,' said Dad.

Sylvie stood up, eyes shining, arms outspread.

'*The passing of the High King*,' she proclaimed and walked slowly upstairs.

'He's turned you stupid,' said Dad.

Sylvie turned on the stairs. Eyes wide, lips slightly parted, she faced them.

'No,' she said. 'Don't you see?'

'That I don't,' said Dad.

She came down the stairs again.

'Think,' she said in a low, quivering voice. 'Visualize the scene. The High King is dead. His warriors place him in his longship for his last journey. They load it with treasure, for he is to stay with the gods. Then, wrapped in grief, heads bowed, they surround his body. With his death, the great age of heroes is gone.

'Then the mound is closed. Soon the warriors themselves enter the great sleep. Sleep and wait. Sleep and wait through the centuries. For they know their leader will return. When the hour is ripe the new great age will dawn. The king will come again in triumph.

'Millennia pass. Then, one Winter Solstice, a tremor runs through the Burial Mound. The sleepers stir. Is it time? Outside, the world celebrates a birth. Can the faithful guardians of the tomb celebrate a rebirth? Urgent messages enter the warriors' tranced minds. Is he here, miraculously preserved? Or is his mighty spirit reincarnated into a new human frame?

'The warriors rise. Their strength returns. The old blood courses through their veins; the old magic still works. Their duty is to bring home their lost leader. He has been guided so far; the last miles are for them. So out into our world they venture, to take a man too great for these times back to his people.

'Oh, Oliver. The *hero*.'

There was a profound silence.

'Bloody hell,' said Dad at last.

'He ate too much to be a hero,' said Matthew.

But Stephanie thought back to the amazing visions he had shared with them while he was in the process of eating too much–that blond giant with the huge voice. Yes, he was larger than life. No, their eyes at the Mounds had not deceived them.

'Sylvie's right,' she said.

Another silence.

'What will you do now, Sylvie?' said Mum.

'Does it matter?' said Sylvie. 'I was his guide. I brought the High King back to his own. That is enough for me.'

She closed her eyes with an expression of sheer bliss and let out a long sigh. The silence intensified.

The doorbell rang. Everybody jumped.

'Go and see who it is, Matthew,' said Mum.

Matthew did and a moment later everyone shared his gasp of shock.

Oliver. Once again in his modern walking gear, smothered in mud, drenched to the skin, blue eyes rolling in his face. His open mouth took in great gulps of air.

'You poor man,' cried Mum. 'You must get those filthy things off and have a shower.'

Oliver's eyes met Sylvie's. She screamed and fainted. As Oliver was hustled upstairs Dad saw the last of his brandy go.

But Matthew was looking beyond where Oliver stumbled in—way into the dark outside. For a second he was sure he saw two huge blond warriors standing in the road. Light from the streetlamps flashed gold off their armour. Their faces were creased with contempt and they shook their spears in rage. And disappeared.

Back in the house, everyone waited. From upstairs came the noise of the shower; then a long period of quiet. Sylvie sat again in the armchair, her eyes wide and round.

Eventually Oliver appeared, carrying a suitcase. He was changed utterly. He wore a very sharp oatmeal suit, silk shirt, and hand-knitted tie. His soft leather Italian shoes must have cost a fortune. His beard had gone and aftershave wafted from his pink, smooth cheeks.

'I can't understand it,' he said. 'Every Winter Solstice it's the same. I never seem to get it quite right.'

They stared at him. He went on.

'I had just this trouble last year at Glastonbury.'

He turned to Sylvie.

'So it's goodbye,' he said. 'We made a mistake. Still, win some, lose some, that's what I say.'

Sylvie looked at him, speechless.

'Cheerio, then,' he said. 'I'll find my own way to the station.'

He closed the front door behind him. Still nobody said a word. Then Mum moved. She dashed to the front door, opened it and shouted down the road.

'You can't just walk out like that. What about poor Sylvie? What do you think you're doing?'

The answering cry came from fifty yards away.

'I'm going to get myself a woman with relatives in St Albans, York, or Chester. It looks like decadent Roman orgies are more in my line after all. And someone's got to find the lost Legion for them.'

Court Martial

Charles C. O'Connell

He stood pallid and tense before the officers. Though he was now unarmed and shorn of all his field equipment, his tunic seemed to drag heavily on his shoulders, and the weight of his helmet was almost unbearable; he could hardly keep his head erect. His right arm, which had been twisted viciously behind his back, hung limply by his side, numb and lifeless, except for the faint pulse that beat under his arm-pit.

He stood with his feet apart, although years of discipline urged him to stand to attention, but he knew that if he did so he would topple over. In fact, it made no difference how he presented himself; the verdict of the court martial would be 'guilty'. He had disobeyed orders. Only his own conscience could justify his action. According to their code, he was a rebel... Well, let it be. If he had to relive the episode, he would do exactly the same thing.

The heat inside was quite intolerable. He longed to step back a little into the current of air that moved the canvas by the door, yet he dared not. Such an action might antagonize his judges even more, and although he could see no vestige of mercy or even humanity in their stern faces, he had hope that perhaps, in spite of everything, they would understand.

'You have heard the evidence.' The voice of his superior officer jarred on his ears. 'Have you anything to say?'

The prisoner thought for a moment. Had he anything to say in his defence? No, he had not—nothing that they could understand. But what could he not say of this useless bloodshed, which was for assassins rather than soldiers! This war on women and innocent children was repugnant to him. Nothing, he thought, could justify this mass murder, yet to say so here would be treason.

'Answer!' snarled the officer.

'I have nothing to say.'

'Do you deny that you allowed those refugees through?'

Perhaps it would be better if he said something–anything to shorten the farcical trial. 'I let them through,' he said hoarsely, admitting the charge for the first time.

The officer smiled. 'Against your specific orders?'

'Yes.'

Why in the name of glory did they persist in this mockery?

The two officers held a whispered consultation. One of the guards behind the prisoner shuffled for an instant and was still again. Then the second officer spoke. His was a soft face with none of the harsh lines of his superior, but his eyes were colder than a winter dawn.

'We should be interested to know why you allowed all three to go. Had you done your duty by one, there would have been no further trouble. Were they friends of yours? Did you know them? Or were you tempted by the amount of the bribe?'

The prisoner shook his head, and the perspiration temporarily held by his eyebrows trickled to his chin. 'They offered no bribe, sir. I did not know them.'

'Then why did you let them through?'

'I thought it was—just.'

'What do you know of justice?' the officer sneered.

The prisoner closed his eyes. Once again the picture of those three weary travellers came to his mind. They were fleeing from a terror which he represented. He had not harmed them because they looked so desperately tired, or perhaps it had been that heart-searching appeal in the young woman's eyes, or perhaps it was because of the child, so helpless in a world gone mad... Whatever the reason, his orders had suddenly appeared monstrously evil.

He opened his eyes. 'I am a soldier,' he said firmly. 'I will not become an assassin.'

And then the guard behind him struck him at the base of the neck and he slumped to the ground. He was vaguely conscious of being kicked, but it did not hurt any more. A strange sense of unreality possessed him, as though he existed only in a dream.

Some time later, he found himself on his feet again. The business of the court had finished. There had been no death sentence. One of the officers merely nodded his head to the guard, and the prisoner was propelled towards the door.

He staggered as he came into the sunlight, and his helmet fell off. Nobody picked it up—he would have no further use for it. The cool air stirring through his matted hair was as invigorating as wine. He was rushed forward and then, some paces from the door behind a high, screening boulder, his guards stopped.

The prisoner was under no illusion. He knew that in a few moments he would be dead. Yet he had no regrets. Perhaps it would be better to leave this world of unjustice and suffering.

Vaguely, he wondered if it would always be like this. That could hardly be possible. Men must one day realize the futility of bloodshed. Perhaps, in a thousand or two thousand years, men would have at last learnt to live in peace and there would be no greed, nor wars, nor murder.

He stood erect. He did not feel afraid. He was filled with a strange, new hope. He thought of those three travel-stained refugees. He hoped they got through to Egypt. Once there, the child would be safe from Herod's barbarous assassins...

Acknowledgements

The following stories were specially commissioned for this book and are reprinted by permission of the Author unless otherwise stated:

'Brown Baby' copyright © Gwen Grant 1986 by permission of the Author and David Higham Associates Ltd. 'Lost Leader' copyright © Dennis Hamley 1986. 'The Christmas Present' copyright © Kathleen Hersom 1986. 'Get Lost' copyright © Robin Klein 1986 by permission of the Author and Curtis Brown (Aust) Pty Ltd, Sydney. 'Burper and the Magic Lamp' copyright © Robert Leeson 1986. 'The Anarchist's Pudding' copyright © Geraldine McCaughrean 1986. 'The Christmas Gift' copyright © Hugh Oliver 1986. 'A Christmas Pudding Improved with Keeping' copyright © Philippa Pearce by permission of the Author and Laura Cecil. 'A Lot of Mince-pies' copyright © Robert Swindells 1986. 'Call Me Blessed' copyright © Jacqueline Wilson 1986 by permission of the Author and Murray Pollinger.

The editor and publishers gratefully acknowledge permission to reproduce the following copyright material:

George Mackay Brown: 'The Lost Boy' from *Andrina and other Stories* by George Mackay Brown. Reprinted by permission of the Author and Hogarth Press. Timothy Callender: 'An Assault on Santa Claus' from *It So Happen* by Timothy Callender. Reprinted by permission of the Author and Christian Journals Ltd., Belfast. Nicholas Fisk: 'Ghost Alarm' copyright © Nicholas Fisk 1986. Reprinted by permission of the Author and Laura Cecil. John Gordon: 'The Ivy Man' copyright © John Gordon 1986. Reprinted by permission of the Author. Shirley Jackson: 'A Visit to the Bank' from *Life Among the Savages* by Shirley Jackson. Copyright 1945, 1948, 1949, 1950, 1951, 1952, 1953, by Shirley Jackson. Copyright renewed © 1973, 1976, 1977, 1978, 1979, 1980, 1981 by Laurence Hyman, Barry Hyman, Mrs Sarah Webster and Mrs Joanne Schnurer. Reprinted by permission of Farrar, Straus and Giroux Inc. Gerald Kersh: 'The Charcoal Burner' from *Men Without Bones* by Gerald Kersh. Reprinted by permission of the Author and William Heinemann Ltd. Laurie Lee: 'Carol-Barking' from *Cider with Rosie* by Laurie Lee. Reprinted by permission of the Author and the Hogarth Press. Harry Macfie: 'A Christmas Eve' from *Wasa-Wasa*. Reprinted by permission of Allen and Unwin. Jan Mark: 'Welcome Yule' from *The Magnet Book of Sinister Stories*. Reprinted by permission of the Author and Methuen, London. Mabel Marlowe: 'The Snowman'. Reprinted by permission of the Author and Basil Blackwell (Publisher) Oxford. Leslie Norris: 'Sliding' from *Short Stories* by Leslie Norris. Reprinted by permission of the Author, J M Dent and Sons Ltd, and Charles Scribner's Sons. Frank O'Connor: 'Christmas Morning' from *The Stories of Frank O'Connor*. Reprinted by permission of A D Peters and Co Ltd and Joan Davies. James Riordan: 'Grandfather Frost' from *Tales from Central Russia* by James Riordan (Kestrel Books, 1976) copyright © James Riordan, 1976. Reprinted by permission of Penguin Books Ltd. Olaf Ruhen: 'Christmas in the Floods' from *The Cool Man and Other Contemporary Stories by Australian Writers*. Reprinted by permission of the Author and Angus and Robertson Ltd. Norman Smithson: 'A Present for Grannie Fox' from *The World of Little Foxy* by Norman Smithson. Reprinted by permission of the Author and Victor Gollancz, Ltd. Catherine Storr: 'Christmas in the Rectory' from *Ghost after Ghost* edited by Catherine Storr. Reprinted by permission of the Author and Penguin Books, Ltd. Sue Townsend: 'Adrian Mole's Christmas' from *The Secret Diary of Adrian Mole aged 13¾* by Sue Townsend. Reprinted by permission of the Author and Methuen, London. David Henry Wilson: 'Father Christmas and Father Christmas' from *Getting Rich with Jeremy James* by David Henry Wilson. Reprinted by permission of the Bodley Head.

While every effort has been made to secure permission, we may have failed in a few cases to trace or contact the copyright holder. We apologize for any unintentional discourtesy.

We wish you all a very happy and peaceful Christmas.

AND it came to pass, in those days, that there went out a decree from Cæsar Augustus, that all the world should be registered.

(And this registration was first made when Cyrcnius was governor of Syria.)

And all went to be registered, everyone into his own city.

And Joseph also went up from Galilee, out of the city of Nazareth, into Judæa, unto the city of David, which is called Bethlehem (because he was of the house and lineage of David),

To be registered with Mary, his espoused wife, being great with child.

And so it was that, while they were there, the days were accomplished that she should be delivered.

And she brought forth her first-born son, and wrapped him in swaddling clothes, and laid him in a manger, because there was no room for them in the inn.

And there were in the same country shepherds abiding in the field, keeping watch over their flock by night.

And, lo, the angel of the Lord came upon them, and the glory of the Lord shone round about them; and they were very much afraid.

And the angel said unto them, Fear not; for, behold, I bring you good tidings of great joy, which shall be to all people.